Facts & Folklore

An Historical Guide to

Galiano Island

Landmarks, Events, Activities, Parks, Beaches,
Plants & Wildlife, Accommodations,
Restaurants, Shops & Services

Vicky Lindholm

Hidden Lighthouse Publishers

Hidden Lighthouse Publishers
A division of Diskover Office Software Ltd.
Email: info@hiddenlighthouse.com
www.hiddenlighthouse.com

Cover design, page design and composition by Vicky Lindholm
All photos, with the exception of those listed under Credits, by Vicky Lindholm

Front cover photo:
Retreat Cove, Galiano Island

Back cover photo:
Montague Harbour Marina, Galiano Island

ISBN 978-09783367-2-1

Corporate orders:
Granville Island Publishing
www.granvilleislandpublishing.com
604-688-0320
1-877-688-0320

To Ken Smith,
who was kind enough to allow the
inclusion of some of his photos in
this book

Contents

Contents

A Tale of Galiano

Sturdies Bay Wharf

It was in 1901 that an Englishman, named Stanley Page, came to Galiano Island and was given a portion of his father's land...

Stanley Page was born in the 1880's and immigrated with his family to Canada. At the turn of the century, they moved to Galiano Island.[1]

In 1910, Stanley's mother passed away, leaving him and his siblings to be raised by his father, alone.[2] Two years later, Stanley built a home on his portion of the property and brought his bride to live there with him.[3]

In the 1920's, Mr. Stanley Page became **the Postman** for South Galiano. Using a horse and a boat, he moved a little building onto his ranch, from which he operated the post office.[4]

In the 1940's, he became Galliano's only taxi driver. After 30 years of service, he retired at age 89, as the oldest taxi driver in all of Canada.[5] He and his wife had lived on the same property for 60 years.[6]

Later, when speaking about how his father had felt about delivering the mail during his youth, one of his sons had this to say about him:

Dad was much happier working his farm, or building local houses and bridges.

Kenneth Page[7]

Galiano Island

Things to Know

Just sit right back and you'll hear a tale...

Galiano is a scenic island. It lies in the rain shadow of the Vancouver Island Mountains, which protects it from storms that blow in from the Pacific Ocean. Often referred to as the *Banana Belt* of Canada, the Islands have a Mediterranean-type climate, which is warm during the day and cool at night.

Galiano Island enjoys an average of 2,000 hours of sunshine, annually. With the longest frost-free season in the country, spring begins as early as February. Because it rarely snows, a winter weekend on Galiano can be quite cozy with some logs on a *paia* (fire).

At 57 sq km, Galiano is one the largest of the Gulf Islands. Its rolling hills and roads are reminiscent of an English *Illahee* (countryside). There are no traffic lights, no curbs and no sidewalks, making it quite a quaint attraction.

Called *The Jewel of the Strait of Georgia*, Galiano holds claim to having one of the largest provincial parks in all the Gulf Islands. Almost 75 percent of Galiano falls within a tree farm license held by British Columbia's forestry giant.

Most of the Gulf Islands are uninhabited. However, at the time of this writing, Galiano had a population of about 1,000 permanent residents, a large percentage of which are over 55 years of age and retired.

Part-time residents own cottages as their 'home away from home', living as *weekenders* (people who spend weekends on Galiano) during the tourist season. At that time, the population swells to around 4,000.

Sturdies Bay

Residential development began on South Galiano in the 1860's, along the

Galiano Island

waterway that is officially called *Active Passage*, but was then known locally as *Plumper Pass*.[8] The community that developed was named *Sturdies Bay*, in honor of a family who settled there.[9]

Over the next 60 years, the community at the north end of the Island also began to develop. By the 1920's, North Galiano had become one of the most prosperous communities in all the Gulf Islands, growing to several thousand people during the fishing season.[10]

Sturdies Bay in the 1940's – Galiano Archives 2004026512

In the late 1940's, South Galiano acquired its own power company. However, because of the tree farm that exists between the north and south ends of the Island, power was not extended to North Galiano until the 1960's.[11]

By then, the communities on South Galiano had become more populous and, in the 1970's, they experienced a population explosion. When the last cannery on North Galiano closed, only about a dozen families lived there.[12]

Sturdies Bay as it appears today

Galiano Island

Today, Sturdies Bay, on South Galiano, is 'downtown' to the Island residents. It is a seaside village where the residents and businesses co-exist.

Sturdies Bay Wharf

At the turn of the century, a wharf was built at Sturdies Bay. The wharf accommodated ships coming through Active Pass.

There was no railing along the sides of the wharf at that time. Unfortunately, one day, a team of horses, which was pulling a wagonload of bricks, bolted, and then fell overboard and drowned.[13]

Later, in the 1950's, a new wharf was built, to accommodate the ship named *Princess Elaine*. It was built beside the original wharf so the piles could be driven deeper into the ocean floor.[14]

A decade later, a ferry linking the mainland to neighboring Salt Spring Island was introduced, making Galiano more accessible to Vancouver Island and the mainland.[15]

Sturdies Bay wharf in the late 1950's - Galiano Archives 2004026519

Galiano Island

Today, British Columbia Ferry Services uses the land at Sturdies Bay to operate scheduled ferry services from both the mainland and Vancouver Island.

Sturdies Bay wharf as it appears today

Galiano Island Post Office

Before the turn of the century, steamer ships delivered the mail to Salt Spring Island, and then it was delivered to neighboring Mayne Island.[16]

The first *North Galiano Post Office* was operated from a house near a bay on North Galiano.[17] Once a month, an Indian, who called himself 'Captain Peatson', would row to Salt Spring in a canoe and pick up the mail addressed to `North Galiano`.[18] Later, when steamers began to dock in the bay, the mail was retrieved[19] from the crew.

Initially, residents of South Galiano would row to Mayne Island to collect their mail. By the turn of the century, a steamer ship began to deliver mail once a week to the Sturdies Bay wharf. Soon, the *South Galiano Post Office*

began to operate from various homes at the south end.[20]

At that time, there was only a cow trail running between the north and south ends of the Island. If a settler on South Galiano had a package to send to North Galiano, he would use an axe to pin instructions to a tree at the south end of the trail and the next settler on route to North Galiano would carry the instructions on foot or by horseback.[21]

Pack horse at the turn of the century
Galiano Archives M005

By the early 1920`s, mail had ceased to be delivered to North Galiano by steamer. It was simply transferred there once a week from South Galiano.[22] Much later, the house that served as the first North Galiano Post Office was demolished, along with some priceless letters.[23]

In the late 1920's, postal service for South Galiano was transferred to **the Postman** who performed his duties from

GaLiaNo ISLaNd

a little, shingled, post office building on his ranch.[24]

Shortly thereafter, the Royal Canadian Legion decided that a war veteran should fill the position. So **the Postman** lost the post.[25]

Today, the little post office building that was used by **the Postman** still stands in a backyard on Georgeson Bay Road.

South Galiano Post Office, in the 1930's
Galiano Archives 2004020037

The house had originally been a barn. Postal services were performed from a room on the right-hand side of the house, which was entered by way of a little door.[27]

The house served as the fifth post office for several years. It was eventually passed down to a descendant[28] and still stands on Georgeson Bay Road today.

South Galiano Post Office
as it appears today

Soon, the South Galiano Post Office was moved again, to a house that was located about 5 km from the wharf. It was the fifth building to which it had been moved.[26]

Galiano Island

Sorting office at the Sturdies Bay wharf in the 1930's - Galiano Archives M309

In the 1930's, a small building was set up at the Sturdies Bay wharf, for use as a mail sorting office.[29]

The sorting office building was opened an hour before the mail was due to arrive and the settlers would stand and wait at a counter for their envelopes and parcels to be dispatched.[30]

One day, after 15 years of sitting at the wharf, the sorting office building vanished. It was eventually located on another road, where a road crew had moved it.[31]

The following day, it was moved near Sturdies Bay Road, where it remained for two years.[32]

South Galiano Post Office in the 1940's
Donald New 2004020078

Galiano Island

In the 1960's, the government built a little post office out of bricks at Sturdies Bay. It operated until the 1990's, when it was sold. The post office was then moved further north, to a market.[33]

Today, the little brick building operates as an antique and gift store,[34] and the *Galiano Island Post Office* sits in a storefront across the road.

Galiano School & Activity Centre

Initially, the children of South Galiano attended a school near the Pass.[35] The children who lived near the harbour on the western shore had to row to a trailhead, and then walk to the school.[36] So, in the 1890's, a second school was built, on the southwest side of the Island.[37]

In the year 1900, a third school opened, on a bay on the southeast side of the

Island.[38] The students would bring cans of pork and beans to the school, which they warmed on a heater.[39] For a while, church services were also held there.[40]

Five years later, a fourth school was opened further north. Called the *Retreat Cove School*, the tiny school served a community called *Retreat Cove*.[41]

In the year 1920, a prominent settler donated some land for a fifth school, near a cove on the southeast side of the Island.[42]

The fifth school was called the *Galiano School*.[43] It had one room, in the center of which stood an iron stove. At the top of the stairs sat a container of drinking water.[44]

The first school was in use until just after the turn of the century and the third school was eventually demolished.[45]

The fourth school closed in the late 1930's. Although another school opened in the same community after World War II, it was closed three years later when the population of North Galiano began to decline.[46]

By that time, all of the schoolchildren on South Galiano were attending the Galiano School. So a second room and set of stairs were soon added to it.[47]

GaLiaNo ISLaNd

The Galiano School in the 1930's – Galiano Archives 2004026356

In the 1950's, a sixth school was built on South Galiano. It was named the *Galiano School and Activity Center*. Upon its completion, the Galiano School was sold. It is now the home of a hardware and building supplies store.[48]

The Galiano School as it appears today

Today, the Galiano School and Activity Center, which is located on Gardner Road, serves elementary and junior high students on both North and South Galiano. Grade 12 students are transported to schools on neighboring Islands.

NoRtH GaLiaNo CoMMUNity HaLL

During World War I, a log schoolhouse was built on North Galiano.[49] It was called the *North-End School*.[50]

Galiano Island

North End School in 1927
Galiano Archives M204

In the 1920's, the owner of a marine shop built a frame building beside the log schoolhouse. It was called the *North Galiano School*. For the most part, it replaced the log schoolhouse,[51] maintaining an enrollment of about 24 students.[52]

When the Retreat Cove School closed in the late 1930's, the schoolchildren were transferred to the North Galiano School. Their parents rented a cabin for the students to live in while they attended school there.[53]

North Galiano Community Hall in the 1930's - Galiano Archives M204

A decade later, the North Galiano School had four additional windows added to provide more light. In order for them to fit, they had to be placed in a staggered formation between the existing windows,[54] which gave the building a unique characteristic.

When the North Galiano School closed in the 1950's, the schoolchildren were transferred to the Galiano School on South Galiano.[55] In the 1970's, the North Galiano School became the home of the *North Galiano Community Hall*.[56]

Today, the North Galiano Hall is host to many events, including the annual *Canada Day Jamboree*. It is located on Porlier Pass Road.

Galiano Island

North Galiano Hall as it appears today

Galiano Community Hall

In the 1920's, **the Postman** donated some land beside the Galiano School for the building of a community hall.[57] Upon completion, it was called the *Galiano Community Hall*.[58]

The community hall had a closed porch with a gable. There was a lean-to kitchen with a wood stove at one end and two dressing rooms at the back.[59]

A big steel drum between the windows generated heat. Light was provided by old Coleman mantle lanterns, which hung off the walls and from the ceiling.[60]

The official opening of the community hall was a celebration. Special guests received a royal welcome at the wharf as they arrived by boat.[61]

In the 1930's, the hall was enlarged so that, during the winter, it could accommodate badminton matches and other events. Later, in the 1960's, heaters were installed in the hall, followed by indoor plumbing.[62]

Galiano Community Hall in the 1970's – Galiano Archives M103

Galiano Island

Today, the Galiano Community Hall serves as a venue for various events. It is located on Sturdies Bay Road.

Galiano Community Hall as it appears today

DayStar Market

In the 1980's, a painter moved to Galiano where he and his partner spent a week painting a large garden mural on the side of a mobile market.[63] Later, the market housed the post office.[64]

Today, the market is called the *Daystar Market*. It provides for fresh organic and conventional produce, specialty, health and grocery items, as well as movie rentals. It is located on Georgeson Bay Road.

The Corner Store

In the 1970's, a general store was built[65] in a central location on South Galiano.

The Corner Store in the 1970's - Galiano Archives M065

Today, the store is called *The Corner Store*. It operates as a grocery, liquor and drug store. Located on Georgeson Bay Road, it also provides for movie rentals.

The Corner Store as it appears today

GaliaNo GaraGe & GroceRieS

During World War I, the main road through Galiano was gravel, but made for a relaxing ride. It was not unusual to meet what appeared to be a driverless horse and wagon, only to find that the driver was resting on the floor of the wagon, while his horse navigated his way down the road.[66]

At that time, a horse-drawn carriage with a coachman's box was often seen driving down the Island roads. The carriage was called a 'Victoria'. The settler who owned it had it shipped from England, where it had been driven on London's Rotton Row.[67]

In the 1920's, gasoline-powered engines were introduced to Galiano. Within a few years, there were five Model 'T' Fords being driven around the Island. They put an end to the sight of the Victoria on the road.[68]

Today, you can gas up your *chikchik* (wagon) at *Galiano Garage and Groceries*. In addition to gasoline, you can also purchase groceries and rent movies there. The station is located at Sturdies Bay.

GaliaNo ISLaNd GoLF & CouNtry CLub

Just before the onset of World War I, the settler who drove the horse-drawn Victoria carriage built a house on a farm. The house had a square roof.[69]

In the late 1930's, the house was used as a clubhouse for the first Galiano golf club. A decade later, it was traded for a Jersey cow, and then dismantled.[70]

Galiano Island

Golf Clubhouse in 1940 – Galiano Archives 2004020057

Today, the farm is the site of the *Galiano Island Golf and Country Club*. It offers a challenging 9-hole golf course that features unique sandstone tee markers. Carts and golf clubs are available for rent at the club, which is located on St. Andrews Drive.

Galiano Island Skate Park

In the year prior to this writing, the construction of a skate park began with a set of engineered construction plans and an old B.M.X. racetrack. The cement finishers who constructed it stayed awake all night because the cement refused to harden.[71]

To help pay for the park, a music CD, called 'The Galiano Collection', was recently recorded by Galliano's top musicians.[72] The park, which is called *Galiano Island Skate Park*, is located in Galiano Lions Park on Burrill Road.

Galiano Island

Not the Galiano Island Bank

Treasure Hunt
There is a 3,000 year old Indian fishing village on a beach. Can you find it on Galiano Island?

RCMP Station

Shortly after the turn of the century, police headquarters were moved to Salt Spring Island[73] and constables there became responsible for law enforcement on Galiano.[74]

Today, there are over 6,000 *Queen's Cowboys* (RCMP) employed in British Columbia. However, there is only one constable employed on Galiano. He is stationed on Porlier Pass Road.

Galiano Island Bank

The *Galiano Island Bank* clearly does not exist. However, at the time of this writing, there were Automated Teller Machines (ATM's) at the Montague Marina Grocery, the Corner Store, Galiano Garage and Groceries, and the Hummingbird Inn Pub.

Galiano Island Fire Departments

In the 1950's, the Galiano Chamber of Commerce purchased a Wajax pump and trailer. Along with some other pumps, this equipment was all that existed for fire fighting equipment on Galiano.[75]

A decade later, a pumper truck was purchased from Vancouver Island and an old building, which was originally operated by a power company, was used as a fire hall.[76]

In an effort to pay for the property and equipment, two women designed a large thermometer that displayed 20 equally spaced lines, each representing one hundred dollars. Then, they hung it at Sturdies Bay and asked Galiano land owners for donations.[77]

It is assumed that each time a donation was made, the ladies moved a marker up on the thermometer,[78] a method that is still used to motivate Island residents during fundraising events today.

Within a few weeks, donations to the fire fighter's fund had amounted to over $2,000, exceeding the top line on the thermometer.[79]

At that time, because fires had destroyed so many buildings on Galiano in the first half of the century, it was incorporated into a fire protection district and the *South Galiano Volunteer Fire Department* was born.[80]

Shortly thereafter, a resident offered to let the fire department practice using their equipment by burning down some old buildings on his property on a bay. However, when everyone went for lunch, a tree caught fire and help had to be brought in from Mayne Island to fight it.[81]

When the water tank on the pumper truck ran dry and the tide ran out, the pump in the bay began pumping sand, instead of water. Fortunately, the fire was eventually extinguished.[82]

In the 1970's, the founder of the Corner Store donated some land for a new fire hall.[83] Today, there are two Galiano Volunteer Fire Departments serving North and South Galiano. In the year prior to this writing, the North Galiano Volunteer Fire Department acquired its first new fire engine.[84]

Galiano Island

Galiano Island Health Center

Initially, there was no resident doctor on Galiano. So doctors from Salt Spring Island held a weekly surgery in a house at the Sturdies Bay wharf.[85] Later, in the 1950's, a doctor opened a practice on Galiano, but it closed a decade later.[86]

In the 1970's, the founder of the Corner Store donated his old red panel truck to be used as an ambulance. Stretchers were kept in the post office and in the old fire hall.[87] A decade later, a doctor and his wife purchased an Inn on a bay and began operating it as a medical center.[88]

Today, a resident of Galiano provides medical care from within the *Galiano Island Health Center* on Burrill Road. In addition, the Island provides for massage therapy, acupressure, Reiki, and other healing and preventive alternatives.

Galiano Island Community Library

The *Galiano Island Community Library* is located in a small mall at Sturdies Bay. The library is staffed and managed entirely by volunteers.

First Nations Reserve

Initially, an Indian village that belonged to the *Penelakut* Band resided on a point on North Galiano, called Virago Point. The small *rancherie* (village) was named *xinepsem* (caught by the neck). It consisted of a few permanent houses, which were occupied mainly in the summer for gathering food.[89]

GaLiaNo ISLaNd

Today, the Penelakut First Nation accounts for about 13 percent of the entire *Hul'qumi'num* Indian population.[90] The land on Virago Point is still owned by the band and permission must be attained prior to hiking it.

PLaceS to Stay

In the 1920's, an Englishman purchased some land at the harbour. There, he built a British, colonial-style home.[91]

The following year, he established a resort and opened the rooms on the upper floor of his home to guests. He called his guesthouse *Sutil Lodge*.[92]

A large dining hall was added to the lodge, which also functioned as a games room and as a location in which to hold dances.[93]

Sutil Lodge in the 1920's - Galiano Archives 2004017036

Galiano Island

Eventually, the Englishman built 16 guest cabins along the shore and added a grass tennis court nearby.[94]

He would use a converted fishing boat, called the *Mary Jean*, to row out to the steamers in the Pass, and then transport his guests back to the cabins. They were then given access to small, green, flatbottom boats, with which they could visit nearby coves and islets in the harbour.[95]

Sutil Lodge closed in the late 1940's. However, the family continued to live on the property and, in the 1970's, the cabins were opened to young people in need of affordable housing.[96]

Today, there are some lovely accommodations around Galiano Island. Some of the turn-of-the-century Inns and lodges are still in operation. Many newer facilities also exist, particularly along the southeast and southwest shores of the Island.

Rocky Ridge B&B

The *Rocky Ridge Bed and Breakfast* is a B&B on the western shore of South Galiano. The bed and breakfast is located on Ganner Road. Phone: (250) 539-3387.

Paradise Rock Oceanfront

The *Paradise Rock Oceanfront* is a vacation rental on the western shore of South Galiano. It is located on Ganner Road. Phone: (250) 539-3404

Galiano Island

Dionisio Point Prov. Campground

Dionisio Point Provincial Campground is located on Dionisio Point, the northernmost tip of North Galiano. The campground is open year-round and provides for 30 walk-in campsites. The *Raymond V. Smith Interpretive Trail* connects a tidal lagoon at the point with the campground.

Dionisio Point Campground can only be reached by boat. However, there is also a seasonal water taxi that transports visitors to the campground, from the community of Spanish Hills on North Galiano.

Cliffhouse Cottage & Treehouse B&B

The *Cliffhouse Cottage* and *Treehouse B&B* are cottage rentals on the western shore of South Galiano. They are located on Ganner Road. Phone: (250) 539-5239.

Driftwood Village Resort

The *Driftwood Village Resort* offers cottage rentals on South Galiano. They are located on Bluff Road. Phone: 1-888-240-1466

Whaler Bay Lodge

The *Whaler Bay Lodge* is a bed and breakfast guesthouse on the eastern shore of South Galiano. It offers a private dock, as well as kayaks and other small water craft. The guesthouse is located on Cain Road. Phone: 1-877-539-3199

GaLiaNo ISLaNd

BeLLHoUSe INN

At the turn of the century, a settler wearing a Stetson hat came to Galiano, where he purchased a farm called *Active Pass Stock Ranch*. On the farm was a little log home, which he enlarged to accommodate his big family.[97]

In the 1920's, his son took over the house and farm. With the help of his stepmother, he converted the house into a nine-bedroom lodge, called the *Farmhouse Inn*.[98]

The lodge had a main dining room. To polish the dining room floor, it became the custom for one person to sit on a pair of old long johns, while the other family members spun them around.[99]

Guests of the lodge arrived by steamer and were brought from the wharf to the lodge in a converted fishing boat.[100]

Treasure Hunt
There is a plaque commemorating a couple who once owned the land in Bluffs Park. Can you find it in Bluffs Park?

When there was no vacancy at the Inn, they were put up on a point, in tents that had wooden floors and walls.[101]

The guests were free to explore the farm and often helped with the haying. The son would use his steam launch to take them on errands to the wharf or to the other Islands.[102]

A few years after it opened, the lodge caught fire. The son ran through the building in search of people who might need rescuing. When he found no one inside, he seized a vase on his way out. It was the only item that was saved from the fire. Subsequently, the Inn was destroyed and a new one had to be built.[103]

The new home had more bedrooms, and a larger kitchen and dining room. It had its own power plant and was the first home on Galiano ever to receive electricity.[104]

For many decades, the son and his own family operated the Inn. Their boats, the *Betsy Prig* and the *Betsy*, took guests to and from the wharf.[105]

GaLiaNo ISLaNd

The Bellhouse Inn in the 1950's - Galiano Archives 2004026107

The property was sold in the 1960's. The new owners used the house as their private residence.[106] Later, it was used as a medical center.[107]

Later, in the 1990's, a couple purchased the property and renovated it. Then, they reopened it as the *Bellhouse Inn*.[108]

Today, the Bellhouse Inn is operated as a bed and breakfast. The B&B is located on the southern shore of South Galiano, on Bellhouse Road. Phone: 1-800-970-7464

The Bellhouse Inn as it appears today

Galiano Island

Bodega Ridge Lodge & Cabins

Bodega Ridge Lodge and Cabins is located on North Galiano, on Manastee Road. It offers seven log cabins. Phone: (250) 539-2677.

Casa Galiano B&B

Originally known as *The Round House*, the *Casa Galiano Bed and Breakfast* is located near Montague Harbour, on Montague Park Road. Phone: 1-866-824-8093

Montague Harbour Prov. Campground

Montague Harbour Provincial Campground is located in a marine park on the western shore of South Galiano. It provides for 40 campsites that are adjacent to a white shell beach on the harbour. The campground is located on Montague Park Road.

Active Pass Caboose

In the 1970's, a turn-of-the-century Canadian Pacific Railway caboose was barged to Galiano from the mainland. She was then restored and converted into a cottage, complete with a miniature train station.

Today, the caboose is a cottage rental, called the *Active Pass Caboose*. It is located on South Galiano, on Mary Anne Road. Phone: (250) 539-2316

GaLiaNo ISLaNd

Top O' the Heap

The *Top o'the Heap Bed and Breakfast* is a B&B on South Galiano. It is located on Georgia View Road. Phone: (250) 539-3345

MooNSHadoWS GUeSTHoUSe

The *Moonshadows Guesthouse* is a B&B on South Galiano. It is located on Georgeson Bay Road. Phone: (250) 539-5544

MorNiNg BeacH B&B aNd Cottage

The *Morning Beach Bed and Breakfast* is a B&B on the eastern shore of South Galiano. It is located on Harper Road. Phone: (250) 539-3053

Galiano Island

Galiano Inn & Spa

In the 1920's, an English family built a large, Elizabethan-style house at Sturdies Bay. They called it *Dunromin.*[109]

A decade later, an English seaman purchased the home and ran it as a resort. He renamed it *Greenways.*[110]

The resort served as the location for many parties, prospering until the end of World War II when new owners subdivided and sold the property.[111] At that time, it was renamed the *Galiano Lodge.*[112]

Galiano Inn & Spa in the 1930's - Galiano Archives 2004021043

The main floor of the lodge consisted of a large living room. It led off a spacious entrance that had a wide Oak staircase. On the second floor were eight bedrooms and a large bathroom with an extra large bathtub.[113]

The grounds, which had extensive rockwork, had been designed to simulate an English courtyard. There was also a riding stable and a tennis court.[114]

Because the main attraction to the lodge was the fishing, the owners built a wharf and float in the bay. Then, they purchased four small boats with gear and rented them to guests by the hour.[115]

In the 1950's, the Galiano Lodge was destroyed by fire, leaving only the brick steps and stone verandah standing. The owners built a single-storied house on the same site and continued to operate it as a resort into the 1960's. Subsequent owners added more rooms to the building.[116]

Today, the Galiano Lodge is known as the *Galiano Inn*. It offers guest rooms, as well as a meeting room with seating for 40 people. Situated at Sturdies Bay, the Mediterranean-style Inn features the *Madrona Del Mar Spa and Wellness Retreat*. The Inn is located on Madrona Road. Reservations are required. Phone: 1-877-530-3939

Island Time 5 Star B&B

The *Island Time 5 Star Bed and Breakfast* is a B&B on the eastern shore of South Galiano. The only Canada Select five star accommodation on

Galiano, it is located on Sticks Allison Road. Phone: 1-877-588-3506

Woodstone Country Inn

The *Woodstone Country Inn* is an award winning Inn located on South Galiano, on Georgeson Bay Road. Phone: 1-888-339-2022

La Berengerie B&B

The *La Berengerie Bed and Breakfast* operates from a French country-style Inn near Montague Harbour, on South Galiano. The B&B is located on

Galiano Island

Montague Road. Phone: (250) 539-5392

Captain's Quarters

In the year 1890, a sea Captain emigrated from England to Galiano. A few years later, he established a farm on a bay on North Galiano. Initially, a simple lean-to with an earth floor served as the family's home.[117]

The following year, the Captain and his son built a log home with dovetailed corners. Because he worked off-Island, he hired a live-in governess for his children. She educated them in a lean-to classroom that was attached to the back of the log house.[118]

Later, the Captain's son inherited the property. He lived in the home for the rest of his life. The building was then left in an abandoned state for several decades, during which time much of the interior rotted away.[119]

In the 1980's, another sea Captain purchased the property. One hundred years after the house was originally built, he began to restore it.[120]

Today, the log home is operated as a cottage rental, called the *Captain's Quarters*. It is located on North Galiano, on McCoskrie Road. Phone: 1-866-539-3625

Ways to Get Around

Before the turn of the century, settlers did a lot of rowing. The distance that a strong settler could row in a few hours amazes modern sailors today. Some settlers rowed to Vancouver Island, and

GaLiaNo ISLaNd

then walked or took a *latleh* (train) to Victoria. Others rowed to *Big Smoke* (Vancouver).[121]

Because of their amazing strength, some settlers held rowing competitions

between Galiano and Mayne Island, across Active Pass.[122]

Early settlers in a rowing competition across Active Pass, Galiano Archives G-66

If you choose to boat in Active Pass today, keep in mind that it is just that – active! All ferry traffic between Vancouver Island and the mainland travels through the passage, making it one of the busiest bodies of water on the entire west coast.

Keep in mind that if you hear five short blasts of a ship's horn, someone's boat is on a collision course with the ship.

Galiano Island

Galiano can be an enjoyable Island to cycle, so another way to get around is by bicycle or scooter. The *Galiano Triathlon*, which takes place each May, includes kayaking, cycling and running.

Keep in mind that there are no shoulders on the roads and, although some appear to be there for casual country riding, many of them are major thoroughfares that the Islanders use to conduct their business.

Galiano Bicycle

Galiano Bicycle is a bicycle repair shop, which also offers bike accessories and rentals. The bicycle shop is located on Burrill Road.

Go Galiano Island Shuttle

If you need to get somewhere quickly, and you do not have your own *island beater* (old car parked on Galiano), you can hail the *Go Galiano Island Shuttle*. Phone: (250) 539-0202

Galiano Island

Gulf Islands Water Taxi

In the 1930's, a man and his uncle ran a boat-taxi service on Galiano. They charged five dollars for an all-day trip to Vancouver Island and two dollars to go to Mayne Island.[123]

Today *Gulf Islands Water Taxi* provides scheduled trips between Sturdies Bay and Salt Spring Island. Phone (250) 537-2510

Retreat Cove Charters

Retreat Cove Charters and Adventure Tours transports visitors to Dionisio Point Provincial Park and to Wallace Island Marine Park. Phone: (250) 539-9981

Seair Sea Planes

Seair Sea Planes offers daily, scheduled, float plane flights between the Vancouver Airport and Montague Harbour. Phone 1-800-44SEAIR

Harbour Air

Harbour Air offers daily, scheduled, float plane flights between the mainland and Montague Harbour. The planes that are used for the flights are called 'Beavers'. Phone: 1-800-665-0212

Sporades Tours

Sporades Tours provides for ecological tours and sightseeing around the Gulf Islands. The tours take place aboard an authentic fishing boat and are captained by a certified skipper. The tour company is located at the Montague

Galiano Island

Marina on Montague Park Road. Phone: 1-877-588 3506

Galiano Adventures

Galiano Adventures offers boat and moped rentals throughout the summer. It is located at the Montague Marina on Montague Park Road. Phone: 1-877-303-3546

Afternoon Sailing Cruises

Afternoon Sailing Cruises offers sailing trips around Galiano and the southern Gulf Islands. Phone: 1-800-970-7464

Gulf Islands Kayaking

Gulf Islands' Kayaking offers year round kayak tours. Lessons, rentals and camping trips are also available. The tour company is located at the Montague Marina on Montague Park Road. Phone: (250) 539-2442

Galiano Island

Galiano Island Sights & Shops

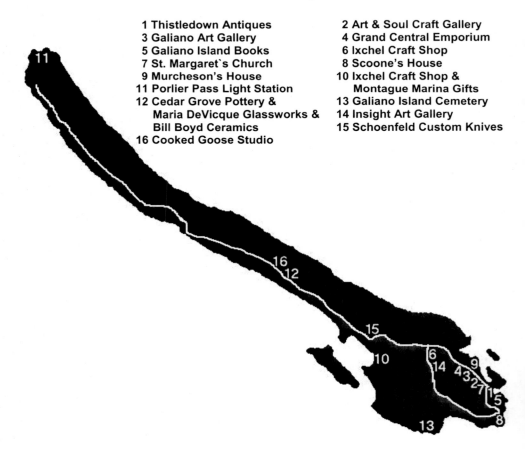

1 Thistledown Antiques
3 Galiano Art Gallery
5 Galiano Island Books
7 St. Margaret's Church
9 Murcheson's House
11 Porlier Pass Light Station
12 Cedar Grove Pottery &
   Maria DeVicque Glassworks &
   Bill Boyd Ceramics
16 Cooked Goose Studio

2 Art & Soul Craft Gallery
4 Grand Central Emporium
6 Ixchel Craft Shop
8 Scoone's House
10 Ixchel Craft Shop &
    Montague Marina Gifts
13 Galiano Island Cemetery
14 Insight Art Gallery
15 Schoenfeld Custom Knives

Galiano Island

Things to See

Galiano Island is a peaceful getaway with numerous areas to explore. Many people come to Galiano simply to camp near the beach, drive through the park or sail out to the lighthouse.

There are only two major routes on Galiano. Porlier Pass Road runs the length of the Island, bisecting it. It connects to Sturdies Bay Road, which leads to the ferry terminal. Sturdies Bay Road turns into Georgeson Bay Road, then into Bluff Road, and then into Burrill Road, circumventing the southern tip of the Island.

St. Margaret of Scotland Church

Initially, Catholic church services were held in a little shed on a South Galiano bay, where a fisherman had previously mended and dried his fish nets.[124] Later, they were held in the old schoolhouse that sat near that same bay. At that time, Galiano was part of the parish of the church on Mayne Island.[125]

During World War I, a woman donated some waterfront property on the bay and a Mission Room was opened there. The altar, organ, lectern, prayer desk and silver communion vessels were all donations.[126] At least once, a baptism was performed in a basin from the kitchen sink in a nearby home.[127]

Shortly thereafter, monthly services on North Galiano began at the Retreat Cove and North Galiano schools.[128] Eventually, the Mission Room was purchased by the Island's undertaker, who made it his home.[129]

Mission Room in the 1950's
Salt Spring Archives 2004026171

In the 1950's, a settler donated some land up the hill, for the building of a proper church. A number of projects were undertaken to raise money for the building of it, including the first *Galiano Art Show*.[130]

Upon its completion, the church was called the *Church of St. Margaret,*

GaLiaNo ISLaNd

Queen of Scotland.[131] A larger-than-life painting of The Crucifixion was hung above the altar.[132] A stained glass window was placed in the rear of the church, in memory of a Reverend who drowned shortly after his appointment to the Gulf Islands' Parish.[133]

For many years thereafter, the owner of a store at Sturdies Bay would stop at the church with his family, on his way to the Saturday night dance. He would light the oil stove in the church so it would be warm for the morning service.[134]

Today, St. Margaret of Scotland Church is the only church on Galiano. It is located on Burrill Road. (#7 on the map)

GaLiaNo ISLaNd CeMetery

Before the 1860`s, Indians buried their dead high in the trees on South Galiano, on a point that is now called Collinson Point. Later, the point became the private burial ground of a very prominent settler.[135]

In the 1920`s, the settler donated the land to be used as the Island's cemetery. He placed two conditions on his donation; that there be no charge for burial of a resident of Galiano and that plots would be reserved there for his own family.[136]

The local undertaker cleared most of the property, which is still surrounded by huge Arbutus and Douglas-Fir trees.[137] The *lych* gate and the fence along one side were both donations.[138]

Galiano Island

The cemetery is accessible from what was once called *Dead End Road*, but was later renamed *Cemetery Road*.[139] (#18 on the map)

Porlier Pass Light Station

Prior to the turn of the century, the passage at the north end of Galiano was called *Cowichan Gap*, but was known locally as *The Gap*.[140] It was later renamed *Porlier Pass*.

> **Treasure Hunt**
> *There are two caves on the west side of a park. Can you find them on Galiano Island?*

At the turn of the century, construction of a major light station began at the Pass. It was called the *Porlier Pass Light Station*.[141]

There were two beacons at the light station, overlooking what is now known as *Lighthouse Bay*. One beacon sat on Race Point and the other sat on Virago Point. Ships navigated the waters by lining up both lights.[142]

The first light keeper was a sailor known locally as 'Sticks'.[143] At dusk, he would light the lamps in each tower so they would burn through the night. In the morning, he would fill the brass coal oil lamps, trim the wicks and polish the chimneys.[144]

Whenever the weather was foggy, he would beat an old tin can to indicate to the boats where the Pass was.[145]

The light keeper served the light station for 40 years. The wicks were in operation in the beacon towers until he retired in the 1940's.[146]

Race Point Tower in the 1950's
Galiano Archives 2004026354

The tower on Race Point was recently removed and replaced with an automated beacon. However, the tower on Virago Point is still standing on the First Nations reserve and can be seen from Dionisio Point Provincial Park. (#11 on the map)

Mary Ann Point Light

In the 1880's, the English seaman who would later own the Galiano Lodge purchased some property on South Galiano. The property sat on a point, called Mary Anne Point. There, he began to build a waterfront home.[147]

At the turn of the century, the seaman moved to England, and then returned after World War I with his fiancé. In the 1920's, he exchanged the property for property owned by his brother.[148] Thereafter, his brother owned the home on the point.[149]

The windows in the home faced a light that sat on the point. It was called the *Mary Anne Point Light*. Fuelled by carbide, it guided the ships through the Pass.[150]

A seaside trail led over flat rock and grass, down to the waters in the Pass, and then through the woods and down the hill to the house and the light.[151]

A garden of wildflowers grew among the rocks, behind which visitors could see the ships sailing through the rough waters.[152]

Mary Anne Point Light, mid 1900's
Galiano Archives M297

In the 1950's, the Mary Anne Point Light was dumped into the sea[153] and the property was sold to a descendant for one dollar.[154]

Galiano Island

Today, a new light stands on the point. It can be seen from the ferries, as they travel through the Pass.

Mary Anne Point Light as it appears today

The 120-year old home that once belonged to the seaman still stands nearby. The house was first enlarged in the 1920's. Subsequent owners have made numerous modifications to it.[155] (#8 on the map)

The Oldest House on Galiano

In the 1880's, a Scotsman came to South Galiano and purchased some land on Sturdies Bay. There, he established a farm on which he built a square-timbered home.[156]

The Scotsman's eldest son was the first white child to grow up on Galiano. When the son drowned at the turn of the century, his younger brother inherited the family farm.[157]

The young brother eventually married and became the father of seven children, which earned him the nickname 'Father Finlay'.[158]

Later, he became a roads foreman for Galiano and many of the roads on the Island were staked out under his supervision.[159]

GaLiaNo ISLaNd

Oldest house on Galiano, in the 1960's – Galiano Archives 2004026157

Today, the Galiano Island Golf Course sits on part of the family's old farm.[160] Their 125-year old home can still be seen from Sturdies Bay Road. It is the oldest house on Galiano.[161] (#9 on the map)

A single-storey kitchen addition was constructed just before the outbreak of World War I. The outside chimney was constructed much later, around the 1950's. However, the house is still very much the way it was at the turn of the century.[162]

Galiano Island

Places to Eat

Around the turn of the century, a settler developed a reputation for being a good cook. Coincidentally, some of the fishermen in the neighborhood began visiting him around mealtime. So the settler devised a plan to cure them of the habit, and then invited them to dinner.[163]

When the fishermen sat down to eat, a large meat pie was set on the table. When the settler cut into it, the fishermen were disappointed to see that it was filled with sawdust and rags.[164]

The settler then brought out a steaming cloth bag. He told the fishermen that it was covering a hot plum pudding. However, when he removed the bag, he revealed a pumpkin shell, instead.[165]

After dinner, the fishermen watched the settler pour each of them some amber-colored liquid. When they drank it, they discovered that it was cold tea.[166]

Today, whatever you hunger or thirst for, there are some good restaurants on Galiano Island where you can get great *muckamuck* (food) and drink.

Woodstone Country Inn Restaurant

The *Woodstone Country Inn Restaurant* offers four-course dinners in its award-winning Wisteria Dining Room. The restaurant, which features contemporary Canadian cuisine, is located on Georgeson Bay Road. Phone: 1-888-339-2022

The Clubhouse Cafe

The Clubhouse Cafe is a licensed restaurant that offers lunch and dinner. Located at the Galiano Island Golf and Country Club, the café also provides for live entertainment.

A summer feature of the restaurant is the Friday Night Nine & Dine, in which golfers can play nine holes of golf and then sit down to a barbecued dinner. Phone: (250) 539-5533

Grand Central Grill Restaurant

In the year prior to this writing, the owners of a gift shop converted their deck into a diner. They called it the *Grand Central Grill Restaurant*.

The 50's-style diner is located at Sturdies Bay and offers breakfast, lunch and dinner. Live entertainment is also provided. Phone: (250) 539-9885

Hummingbird Inn Pub

The *Hummingbird Inn Neighborhood Pub* is a pub and restaurant with an extensive menu. The restaurant also provides for live entertainment.

Atrevida Restaurant

The *Atrevida Restaurant* is a gourmet dining room that focuses on the tastes of the Pacific Northwest. Live entertainment is also provided. Reservations are available. Phone: (250) 539-3388.

Every evening, a nostalgic school bus provides transportation between the restaurant and Montague Harbour. The restaurant is located at Sturdies Bay. Phone: (250) 539-5472

Galiano Island

Trinconmali Café Bakery & Bistro

The *Trinconmali Café Bakery, Deli and Bistro* is a busy morning stop for pastry and coffee. It is located in a small mall at Sturdies Bay. Phone: (250) 539-2004

The Harbour Grill Restaurant

The *Harbour Grill Restaurant* is a licensed restaurant that serves breakfast, lunch and barbeque dinners during the summer. It is located at the Montague Marina on Montague Park Road. Live entertainment is provided. Phone: (250) 539-5733

Daystar Market Cafe

The licensed *Daystar Market Café*, on Georgeson Bay Road, serves lunch and gourmet dinners. It also offers an espresso and organic juice bar. Phone: (250) 539-2800

La BereNgerie ReStauraNt

The *La Berengerie Restaurant* is a French restaurant on Montague Road. In the summer, it features an outdoor vegetarian café. Reservations are required. Phone: (250) 539-5392

PLaceS to SHoP

In the 1920's, a grocery store was built at the head of the Sturdies Bay wharf. The store changed owners twice, eventually becoming *Heryet's Store*.[167]

Heryet`s Store in the 1920's
Galiano Archives 2004017021b

In the 1930's, the store was sold to a witty Irishman, who became its new storekeeper.[168] Later, he turned the store over to his son.[169]

In the 1950's, the Irishman's son purchased and enlarged a building that housed a coffee shop just up the road. Then, he moved the store there.[170] A

decade later, he incorporated the business as *Bambrick's Stores Ltd.*[171]

In addition to a grocery department, the new store now contained a coffee bar and butcher shop on the main floor and a hardware department on the lower floor.[172]

In the year 1970, a fire destroyed the store. The sound of exploding paint cans could be heard from far away.[173] All that remained was the chimney.[174]

Today, shops, studios and art galleries provide visitors to Galiano Island the opportunity to pick up a *potlatch* (gift) for themselves or for *tillicum* (friends). Galiano is home to many fine artists, writers and artisans.

Galiano Island

Many art studios keep extended hours during the self-guided *Galiano Art Studio Tour*, which allows visitors to see the work of artisans in their studios during the summer.

A Studio Tour map, which is published by the Trincomali Community Arts Council, displays the locations of the participating studios. Watch for road signs and the chance to meet an artist working in their studio.

Schoenfeld Custom Knives

Schoenfeld Custom Knives is a studio that offers knives, utensils and pens created by a master knife maker. The studio is located near Montague Harbour, on Clanton Road. (#15 on the map)

Art & Soul Craft Gallery

The *Art & Soul Craft Gallery* provides for artwork, jewelry, candles, soaps, gifts and clothing. It is located in a small mall at Sturdies Bay. (#2 on the map)

Cedar Grove Pottery

Cedar Grove Pottery, on Porlier Pass Road, is a studio that offers raku, stoneware and sculptures produced by local artists. (#12 on the map)

GaLiaNo ISLaNd

GraNd CeNtraL EMporiuM

In the 1890's, an Englishman immigrated to Canada. Three years later, he came to Galiano and purchased some property on a bay near the Pass. There, he established a farm. Later, his older brother moved to the Island and helped him run his farm.[175]

Because settlers initially had to row to Mayne Island for supplies,[176] the brothers were forever lending merchandise to their neighbors. So, at the turn of the century, the older brother built a store near the water. He called it *Burrill Bros. Store*.[177]

Three years later, he built a larger store on the same property and the first store was then used as a shed.[178] While he ran the farm, the younger brother tended to the store.[179]

The store became a gathering place for the Islanders and, for many years, it had the only telephone on the Island.[180] The brothers hung a Swiss cowbell over the door, which their customers rang for service.[181]

Initially, the brothers used a sled pulled by a team of oxen to deliver large orders around the valley. Later, they purchased an old rheumatic horse to serve that purpose, which they hoisted up with a block and tackle each morning.[182]

Eventually, they added a post office, library and gas pumps to the store.

They also added an apartment above the building, which they rented out.[183]

In the 1940's, they sold the store. Subsequent owners dragged it further north, and then added a false front to it.[184] The building has changed owners many times over the years.

Today, the building is the home of the *Grand Central Emporium* gift store. Known locally as the *Old Burrill Store*, it is located at Sturdies Bay, on Sturdies Bay Road. (#4 on the map)

GaLiaNo Art GaLLery

The *Galiano Art Gallery* offers unique and original works by regional artists. In the year prior to this writing, it moved into a newly built complex at Sturdies Bay, on Sturdies Bay Road. (#3 on the map)

Ixchel Craft Shops

Formerly a taco stand, the *Ixchel Craft Shop* opened for business in the year 1990, on Georgeson Bay Road. It offers artwork, stained glass, soaps, chimes, pottery and jewelry made by local artists. (#6 on the map)

A second seasonal outlet is located at the Montague Harbour Marina on Montague Park Road. (#10 on the map)

Bill Boyd Ceramics

In the year 1970, an artist began making pottery in Sweden. Today, he lives and works on Galiano, using four different porcelain and stoneware clays from the Pacific Northwest.

The artist's studio is called *Bill Boyd Ceramics*. Located on Porlier Pass Road, it offers hand-made pottery, which is fired in electric and gas kilns. (#12 on the map)

Galiano Island

Maria DeVicque Glassworks

Maria DeVicque Glassworks is a charming studio on Porlier Pass Road. It offers fine glassware. (#12 on the map)

Galiano Island Books

Galiano Island Books is an impressive bookstore at Sturdies Bay, which offers over 15,000 titles. It also carries art supplies. The bookstore is located on Madrona Road. (#5 on the map)

Thistledown Old & Odd Antiques

Located in a building that was once the home of the post office, *Thistledown Old and Odd Antiques* offers pottery, jewelry and handcrafted items by local artists. It is located at Sturdies Bay, on Madrona Road. (#1 on the map)

Insight Art Gallery

In the year prior to this writing, the *Insight Art Gallery* opened on South Galiano. It features a collection of works by local artists, with displays in glass, sculpture, painting, ceramics, mosaics and textiles. The gallery is located on Georgeson Bay Road. (#14 on the map)

Events to Attend

Early settlers celebrated Queen Victoria's birthday by holding events in the month of May,[185] such as foot and potato sack races. They called the holiday 'May Day'.[186]

Another popular event held during the festivities was the Maypole Dance, which was performed by Galiano Island schoolchildren.[187]

Maypole Dancing in 1929 - Galiano Archives M176

GaLiaNo ISLaNd

Whether it is an annual event, such as the *Galiano Wine Festival* or the *Canada Day Jamboree*, or a special event, such as a music festival or play, there is always something to take in on Galiano Island.

The Galiano Island Lions Club has been active for over 30 years.[188] Together, with the Galiano Island Volunteer Firefighter's Association, it hosts a variety of events throughout the year.

ModerN ANtiqueS SaLe

The *Modern Antiques Sale* is an annual event that is held in April at the North Galiano Community Hall on Porlier Pass Road.

SeaFood DINNer & DaNce

The all-you-can-eat *Seafood Dinner* is held each year at the Galiano Island Lions Club on Burrill Road. The annual seafood buffet includes dancing, raffles, auctions and door prizes.

GaLiaNo FuN TriathLoN

> **Treasure Hunt**
> There is a plaque that commemorates all those who fought for Canada. Can you find it on Galiano Island?

A few years prior to this writing, two women started an event, called the *Galiano Fun Triathlon*. The triathlon takes place each May in Montague Harbour Park, on Montague Park Road. It involves kayaking, cycling and running.

Recently, over 120 people took part in the event. The oldest competitor was 76 years old when he participated in his first triathlon. He had not ridden a bicycle in almost 60 years.

Saturday Market

The *Saturday Market* is held every Saturday, from June to September. It features locally produced art and crafts, foods and fresh produce. The market is held at the Galiano Island Lions Club on Burrill Road.

Galiano Island

Canada Day Jamboree

The *Canada Day Jamboree* is held each year on July 1, at the North Galiano Community Hall on Porlier Pass Road. It provides for a colorful parade and fair.

Galiano Art Show

At the turn of the century, a school-aged boy moved with his family from Mayne Island to Galiano.[189]

The boy loved to draw. As he grew older, he learned how to paint. He would make paints by grinding color out of berry juice and earth pigments. Sometimes, he would buy paints from the brothers who ran the Burrill Bros. Store at Sturdies Bay.[190]

At the turn of the century, the budding artist and his family moved to the mainland where he became a well-known painter.[191]

In the late 1940s, the painter returned to Galiano and built a home and studio, where he spent summers with his own family. Shortly thereafter, he sponsored the first *Galiano Art Show*.[192]

It was at his studio that he painted an interpretation of The Crucifixion. It was hung in St. Margaret's Church, where a memorial service was held for him after his death in the 1960's.[193]

Today, the Galiano Art Show is hosted by the Artists Guild of Galiano. The event is held each year in July.

GaLiaNo ISLaNd

GaLiaNo FieSta

The Galiano Fiesta is an annual event that provides for a barbecue, beverage garden, craft booths, games and exhibits. A feature of the event is the Gumboot Toss. There is also a colorful parade.

Sponsored by the Galiano Island Lions Club, the Galiano Festival takes place on July 31, in Galiano Lions Park on Burrill Road.

GaLiaNo WiNe FeStivaL

Treasure Hunt
A plaque reads,
Ed Lee
Gone to Sea
Can you find it on
a beach?

The *Galiano Wine Festival* is an annual event held in August. The event allows visitors to the Island to sample wines from around the world.

The festival, which is held in Galiano Lions Park on Burrill Road, provides for music, great food and other activities.

Galiano Island

Roddy Wilson Tournament

The annual, memorial *Roddy Wilson Slow Pitch Tournament* is held in the fall, in Galiano Lions Park on Burrill Road.

Halloween Howl

The annual *Halloween Howl* is held on Halloween. It provides for games, as well as prizes for the best costume. A fireworks display is also provided, in Galiano Lions Park on Burrill Road.

Christmas Celebrations

Every Christmas Eve during World War I, the light keeper at Porlier Pass would make two huge Christmas puddings. He would tie them in large pillowcases and boil them all day in an old fashioned, copper wash-boiler. Then, he would make two big jugs of brown sugar sauce to pour over them.[194]

When the puddings were ready, he would row out to the Indian reservation and serve pudding to each Indian family on a platter. Then, he would serve it to the Japanese-Canadians.[195]

Today, residents of Galiano start the Christmas season off with a Christmas craft fair and market.

The season continues as the Bellingham Central Lions Club, in Washington State, loads the *Christmas Ship* with toys and gifts, and sends it to Galiano.

Known locally as the *Santa Ship*, the ship is greeted at Montague Harbour, and then Santa and his 'helpers' distribute gifts to the kids.

Galiano Island

Galiano Island Parks & Beaches

1 Dionisio Point Prov. Park
2 Spanish Hills
3 Spotlight Cove
4 Shaw's Landing
5 Bodega Ridge
6 Retreat Cove
7 Pebble Beach
8 Garner Road Beach
9 Montague Harbour Prov. Park
11 Morning Beach
12 Cain Peninsula
14 Bellhouse Prov. Park
15 Twiss Road Beach
16 Matthews Point Reg. Park
17 Galiano Bluffs Park
18 Georgeson Bay

Galiano Island

Parks to Visit

Galiano Island has fewer parks than most of the other Gulf Islands. However, what it lacks in number it makes up for in splendor.

Galliano's mature forests are dark with Western Red Cedar, Red Alder, Giant Sword-Fern and Oregon Grape, making for excellent hiking. The trails range from seashore-access, walking trails to forest hikes, so you might want to invest in a pair of *waffle stompers* (hiking shoes).

As well as ensuring that nothing is left on the trails, hikers should take as much of their *iktas* (belongings) as possible off the Island.

Bellhouse Provincial Park

Bellhouse Provincial Park was named after the family who originally built the Bellhouse Inn. They bequeathed the property to the province in the 1960's.[196]

Treasure Hunt
There is a rock with the inscription
PORJUSII
Can you find it on Galiano Island?

Bellhouse Park sits on a rocky peninsula, on the south side of Galiano. It slopes to the sea at the entrance to the Pass.

The park provides for wonderful sandstone and limestone formations on the shoreline around the Pass. Whale sightings are frequent there, and Sea Lions and Harbour Seals are in abundance. There are facilities for picnics if you want to stay awhile.

Galiano Island

Accessible from Bellhouse Road, the park is one of the most scenic in all the Gulf Islands. (#14 on the map)

Treasure Hunt

There is a life-sized stone carving of a man's head, which is resting on a mound of rocks. Can you find it on Galiano Island?

BLUFFS Park

At the turn of the century, the settler who would later be seen driving a horse-drawn Victoria carriage around Galiano emigrated from England.[197] He brought 11 Belgian people with him.[198]

Soon, the settler purchased some land on Galiano, which was occupied by high bluffs that overlooked the Pass. There, he established a farm, called the *Valley Farm*.[199]

In the year 1910, his daughter became the first white child born on Galiano.[200] Later, when one of his Belgian helpers went into labor, he delivered her baby, with the help of a first aid book that was written in Spanish.[201]

In the 1920's, the settler returned to Europe to live. After World War II, he and his wife sold the bluffs to the Galiano Island Development Association. The land was then passed to the Galiano Club and a park was opened there.[202]

Bluffs Park sits in a beautiful, dark, old-growth forest on the southwest side of Galiano. There are 4 km of easy trails, which wander through the park.

The trails lead to a ridge that provides for views across the Pass and down the Channel. They are accessible by way of Bluff Road, which is dotted with some of the largest Western Red Cedar trees in all the Gulf Islands. (#17 on the map)

Galiano Island

Bodega Ridge Provincial Park

Bodega Ridge Provincial Park is located on the northwest side of Galiano. Within the park boundaries, a 4 km long ridge, called *Bodega Ridge*, rises 328 m above sea level. Below the ridge, can be seen Bald Eagles, Peregrine Falcons and Turkey Vultures.

The easy trail along the ridge loops through a rare coastal habitat of Douglas-Fir and Garry Oak, and is one of the best places to see the Hairy Manzanita shrub.

A viewpoint, called *Lover`s Leap*, provides for a spectacular panoramic view of Salt Spring and Vancouver Islands. The trail is accessible from the end of Cottage Way. (#5 on the map)

Centennial Community Park

Centennial Community Park is a small recreational park located on the school grounds on Gardner Road. It provides for a baseball diamond, tennis courts and playgrounds.

Galiano Island

Dionisio Point Provincial Park

Dionisio Point Provincial Park is located on Dionisio Point, the northernmost tip of Galiano. The park is one of the most scenic places on the Island, providing for views of Porlier Pass and Valdes Island.

There are 7 km of easy trails through the park. Two trails, called *Maple Bay Trail* and *Sutil Ridge Loop Trail*, provide access to mature forest in the interior of the park.

Matthews Point Regional Park

Matthews Point Regional Park was established only recently. It provides for a dense forest of mature Douglas-Fir, Arbutus and Garry Oak trees, as well as a stunning beachfront swimming area.

Dionisio Point Park is only accessible by water. However, there is a seasonal water taxi that transports visitors to the park, from the community of Spanish Hills on North Galiano. (#1 on the map)

Galiano Island

The rough trail through Matthews Point Park is accessible from Bluff Road. (#16 on the map)

Montague Harbour Marine Park

In the late 1950's, *Montague Harbour Provincial Marine Park* was the first marine park to be established in all of British Columbia.

Located on the west side of Galiano, Montague Harbour Park provides for lovely forest trails. There are also facilities for picnics if you want to stay a while.

During the summer, British Columbia Parks runs an extensive schedule of free interpretive programs, which are held in the park, at The Meeting Place and at The Marine Park Nature House. The park is accessible from the end of Montague Park Road. (#9 on the map)

Mount Galiano Park

At 300 m, *Mount Galiano* is the highest peak on Galiano. It provides for incredible views of the Gulf Islands and of the San Juan Islands. It is also known for its forest and its spring wildflowers.

Mount Galiano is located in *Mount Galiano Park*, an ecologically sensitive, nature protection area. The 3 km trail

Galiano Island

through the park is of moderate difficulty. It is accessible from Active Pass Drive. (#19 on the map)

Pebble Beach Reserve

In the 1880's, a land survey of Galiano reported the existence of a large beaver dam near a bay on North Galiano. Unfortunately, over the years, the dam disappeared.

Pebble Beach Reserve was recently established as a protected area. It includes rare stands of mature Douglas-Fir. Only recently have the beavers returned to the area to restore the dam.

> **Treasure Hunt**
> *One of the lights from the Porlier Pass Light Station sits on private property. Can you find it on Galiano Island?*

There are three main trails through the reserve, all of which are accessible from the end of McCoskrie Road. (#7 on the map)

The *Cable Bay Trail* and the *Laughlin Trail* are linked by a short interpretive trail, which was set up to contrast a mature forest ecosystem. The trail travels through lands that were once a commercial forest plantation.

The *Laughlin Lake Trail* leads to *Laughlin Lake*, the largest body of water on Galiano. Because it is home to at least 55 species of resident and migratory birds, the lake provides for excellent bird watching.

The *Pebble Beach Trail* travels through a beautiful mature forest and passes *Greig Creek*, *Beaver Creek* and the *Great Beaver Swamp*.

Beaches to Explore

In the 18th century, Commander Dionisio Alcala Galiano led the last Spanish exploration of the British Columbian coast. In the 19th century, an English sea Captain named Galiano Island after this Spanish Commander.[203] Recently, a news columnist discovered a 19th century map, which displayed

GaLiaNo ISLaNd

another island off the coast of British Columbia, whose name was also *Galiano*. The newly discovered island was located 250 miles north of the Galiano of the southern Gulf Islands.[204]

Ironically, the Spanish Commander had named the island of the north several years before the English had named the island of the south after him.[205] Fortunately for southern Gulf Islanders, the Galiano of the north was renamed *Nigei* before the turn of the century.[206]

Today, the Galiano of the south provides for plenty of limestone shoreline and white sand and shell beaches. Its protected bays and shallow waters make it easy to find a

cove to anchor in for the *poolakle* (night).

The scuba diving around Galiano is the best in all of the outer Gulf Islands. Anywhere in Active Pass can be found fish, kelp beds and anemone beds. Keep in mind that much of the scenery in the Pass is at a depth of more than 30 m.

CaiN PeNiNSuLa

In the early 1920's, a man emigrated from Ireland to Canada. When he had borrowed enough money to purchase Gossip Island, off the southeast side of Galiano, he moved his family there.[207]

Although they had no experience living in the bush, the family initially lived in a tent. There was no water on the Island so the man rowed to Galiano every day to fetch water from a spring. Later, **the Postman** helped him dig a well and build a log cabin on his property.[208]

Soon, the man decided to start a resort. So he built some self-contained cottages on the property, each with its own bay.[209]

In the late 1920's, he started a hotel on what his family called *Hotel Point*. He called it the *Gossip Island Hotel*.[210] It had 13 bedrooms, a large dining room and a sitting room with a fireplace. It hosted many dances.[211] The man pioneered the

> **Treasure Hunt**
> *There is a giant hand carved from wood. Can you find it on private property on Galiano Island?*

60

Galiano Island

use of propane as fuel for the hotel and, until it became too expensive, the family used it to cook, heat water and run the lights. The toilets ran on saltwater from the ocean.[212]

In the 1930's, **the Postman** built a summer house on the point. It was built hexagonally out of Cedar and had a Cedar shake roof. He also built a turnstile at the entrance to the hotel.[213]

At the beginning of World War II, the hotel was closed down and partially dismantled.[214]

Gossip Island can be seen from the *Cain Peninsula*. Located on the southeast side of Galiano, the peninsula provides protection to an adjacent bay from the winds blowing in from the Georgia Strait.

The rocky beach on the peninsula is dotted with large pieces of driftwood and provides for interesting sandstone formations. Keep in mind that the beach is closed to the harvesting of scallops, mussels, oysters and clams.[215]

If you launch a boat from the Cain Peninsula, you can travel around Gossip Island and the coves nearby. The peninsula is accessible from the end of Cain Road. (#12 on the map)

GaLiaNo ISLaNd

CooK Cove

Around the turn of the century, a settler and his wife purchased some land near a cove. There, they established a farm that had a fine orchard.[216]

The settler was a fisherman. His wife was a midwife who liked to read Western magazines.[217]

Cook Cove was named after this happy couple. It provides for a sandy beach on the southeast side of Galiano. There are two accesses to the beach, both of which are on Sticks Allison Road.

CooN Bay

In the 1860`s, a 57 m passenger steamer, called the *Del Norte*, sank in a bay. The hulk lay undiscovered for one hundred years.[218]

Coon Bay is located on North Galiano, in Dionisio Point Provincial Park. The bay is one of the most beautiful in all the Gulf Islands.

There is a sandy swimming beach on the bay, where the sculpted sandstone, rocky ledges and abundant marine life become exposed at low tide. However, the beach is only accessible by water.

The point, which is covered with small stands of Arbutus and Garry Oak, is an excellent place to see Bald Eagles and to find Sea Stars. The easy trail around the point is called *Porlier Pass Trail*.

If you launch a boat from Coon Bay, keep in mind that high seas can build in Porlier Pass. Further out from the bay, Canoe Islet is a favorite spot for scuba diving, where the wreck of the Del Norte exists. (#1 on the map)

Ganner Road

There is a short trail on the west side of Galiano, which leads to a secluded, pebbled beach. The beach, which is accessible from the end of Ganner Road, provides for views of Wise Island and the Ballingal Islets. (#8 on the map)

Georgeson Bay

In the 1840's, a child ran away from a Scottish school at the age of 14. He then sailed to far away lands as a cabin boy.[219] Later, the Scotsman purchased some land surrounding a bay. There, he built a cabin on the banks of a creek.[220]

In the 1870's, the Scotsman, who had become known locally as 'Scotty', purchased the remainder of the land around the bay. There, he established a farm and built another home.[221]

Around that time, a tinker who lived on Mayne Island was shot to death and his cabin was looted. When a reward was posted by the police[222] Scotty gave evidence against an Indian, called `Indian Tom`. The Indian was later executed as a result of Scotty's testimony.[223]

On returning home one day, Scotty found his wife lying on the floor. Indians had forced poison down her throat. Thereafter, he and his wife were in constant danger from the Indians.[224]

**Georgeson Bay at the turn of the century
Salt Spring Archives MOR42**

In the 1880's, Scotty moved to Mayne Island and became its first lighthouse

GaLiaNo ISLaNd

keeper, providing service to the lighthouse for over 35 years.[225]

In the early 1920's,[226] his family built him a large retirement home at the head of the bay on his Galiano property. Two years later, he retired and the whole family moved into the house. It soon became known locally as the *Big House*.[227]

Georgeson Bay was named after this Scotsman. Located on the southwest side of Galiano, it provides for a rocky beach, which is a great place to see Sea Lions. The beach is accessible by way of Active Pass Drive. (#18 on the map)

Georgeson Bay as it appears today

MattHeWS PoiNt

Matthews Point is located in Matthews Point Regional Park, on the southwest side of Galiano. At low tide, it provides for one of the most beautiful white sand beaches in all the Gulf Islands. The rough trail to the beach is accessible from Bluff Road. (#16 on the map)

MorNiNg BeacH

After World War I, an Englishman purchased some property that included Lion Islet, off the southeast shore of Galiano. He called the property *Lyons*. There, he built a large home.[228]

In the 1920's, the Englishman exchanged the property for property owned by his brother.[229] Thereafter, his brother became the owner of the property.

In the year 1930, the brother leased the property to a family who ran it as a resort. A few years later, he returned to the property and ran it as a resort for another year, himself.[230]

Galiano Island

Lyons on Lion Islet - Galiano Archives 2004021091

During World War II, the property was leased to the YWCA as a summer camp. It then changed owners several times until 1950, when it was operated as a large chicken farm. A decade later, the house was torn down and a new house was built on the property.[231]

Lion Islet can be seen from Salamanca Point, on the southeast side of Galiano. The pebbled beach on the point is called *Morning Beach*. It is accessible by way of a short trail on Ellis Road. (#11 on the map)

GaliaNo ISLaNd

PebbLe BeacH

Cable Bay is located on the northeast side of Galiano. It is well known as a place to find agates and other semi-precious stones. The beach on the bay is called *Pebble Beach*. It is a great place for a *soak* (swim).

The trail to the beach travels through a beautiful forest and passes two creeks. It is accessible from the end of McCoskrie Road. (#7 on the map)

Retreat Cove

Shortly before the outbreak of World War I, a settler immigrated to Canada from Greece. In the late 1920's, he and his wife purchased some property on a cove, where they established a farm.[232]

On their farm, the couple lived in a little house overlooking a Japanese-Canadian owned herring saltery, where the settler worked.[233]

In the 1930's, the settler built a log cabin for his growing family. Because he had many children, he was known locally as 'Papa'.[234]

The settler raised Black Quebec mink on the farm. So his family called the farm the *Seven Sister Fur Farm*. During World War II, the mink became hard to find, so they were forced to sell them at a loss. Eventually, their farm was also sold.[235]

At that time, the area surrounding the cove was a thriving community, with a school, fish saltery and grocery store.[236]

One day, a party was held for all the fishermen at the Japanese owned saltery. During the party, a fire started on the dock.[237]

The fire spread through the saltery and all the stores, offices and homes at the cove. Ironically, the next day, news came of the Japanese attack on Pearl Harbour.[238]

Galiano Island

Retreat Cove is a beautiful cove on the northwest side of Galiano. It provides for views of Salt Spring Island.

Retreat Cove wharf as it is seen today

The beach on Retreat Cove provides for overhanging rocks and a cavern. It is accessible from the end of Retreat Cove Road. (#6 on the map)

A government wharf, which extends into the cove, serves as a water access point. You can launch a boat from the cove and take a relaxing, quiet tour around a nearby island, called *Retreat Island*. However, keep in mind that the

Galiano Island

cove is exposed to westerly winds and the waters behind the Island are shallow.

Shaw's Landing

In the 1870`s, a settler emigrated from England to Galiano.[239] At that time, he became the first man to settle on North Galiano.[240]

Because there was no store in the community, the settler would row to Vancouver Island for supplies. When steamers began stopping in a little bay near his home, he would row out to them, and pick up mail and groceries from one of the crew.[241]

Soon, he became the first person to offer postal service to the other residents of North Galiano.[242] When he died in 1890, one of his sons took over his postal duties.[243]

The settler's son tended to the family orchard and continued his father's postal duties. Over time, he became

adept at building large model sailboats.[244]

In the year 1912, the Postmaster General approved a request for a post office on North Galiano. It was established at the little bay near the settler's home.[245]

Shaw's Landing was named after this family, who provided postal service to North Galiano for several decades. The beach on the bay provides for a seasonal waterfall. It is accessible by way of Porlier Pass Drive, just south of Cook Road. (#4 on the map)

Shell Beach

Montague Harbour was once an ancient Coast Salish Indian village.[246] Originally named *Stockade Harbour*,[247] the waters made history in the 1860's, when the British captured Indians there because of attacks they had carried out on Pender and Saturna Islands.[248]

Galiano Island

Shell Beach at the turn of the century - Galiano Archives 2004021028

One hundred years later, an end-loading wharf was built at the harbour. For the most part, it replaced the wharf at Sturdies Bay.[249] Shortly thereafter, the *Montague Harbour Marina* opened there.

Shell Beach as it appears today

Today, Montague Harbour is one of the most popular anchorages in the Gulf Islands. Located on the southwest side of Galiano, the wharf is used by sea planes and to transport schoolchildren to neighboring schools.

The Gray Peninsula, which is connected to the head of the harbour by a strip of sand and tidal lagoon, provides for a popular, white shell swimming beach, called *Shell Beach*. Underwater excavations are regularly performed there by *Montague Mudsuckers* (archeologists).

The easy 3 km trail that follows the pristine waters around the peninsula is a great place to find clams. It is also a good place to see Great Blue Herons,

GaLiaNo ISLaNd

Kingfishers, Bald Eagles and other birds. The beach is accessible from the end of Montague Park Road. (#9 on the map)

The Montague Harbour Marina offers a wide range of services for boaters. In addition to moorage, fuel and boat rentals, it carries groceries, and camping and fishing supplies. There is also a seasonal restaurant.

If you launch a boat from the wharf, you can circumnavigate a group of privately owned islands located in the harbour. The Ballingal Islets, at the northwest end of the group, make for an interesting destination.

Treasure Hunt
A plaque on a bench reads,
'Well, Tomorrow`s Another Day'
Can you find it on a beach?

SpaNiSH HiLLS

At one time, North Galiano had a sawmill, six salmon and herring canneries, and a marine shop, called *Baines Motor Boat Repair Shop*. The owner of the marine shop built the North Galiano School, which was also located nearby.[250]

In the 1940's, the post office at Shaw`s Landing was moved up the Island, to a store that had been opened at the turn of the century.[251]

The post office operated from inside the store and there were living quarters in

GaLiaNo ISLaNd

the back.   The store's new owners changed the name to *Clutterbuck's Store.*[252]

A decade later, the store was destroyed by fire and was rebuilt. At that time, it was named the *North Galiano Store.*[253]

**Store at Spanish Hills in the 1950's
Galiano Archives M207**

The store changed owners many times. In the 1960's, it was renamed the *Spanish Hills Store.*[254]   It is now a private residence on Porlier Pass Road.

Store at Spanish Hills as it appears today

Today, the community of *Spanish Hills* provides mainly for wonderful scenery and great sports fishing.   The government wharf that extends into the Channel is owned by the Department of Fisheries.

The beach at Spanish Hills is accessible by way of Porlier Pass Road. (#2 on the map) The area is a great spot for scuba diving at a depth of up to 30 m. The waters further north provide for some spectacular underwater scenery. Keep in mind that currents there can run up to 7 knots.

Galiano Island

Spotlight Cove

At the turn of the century, a seaman owned a small boatyard in a cove. With the help of the model sailboat builder who lived at Shaw's Landing, he transformed a 50-year old dugout canoe into a sailing vessel.[255]

The seaman strengthened the hull of the canoe with an Oak frame and added a cabin, floorboards, decking, a 135 kg keel, three masts and two watertight bulkheads. He called the vessel the *Tilikum*.[256]

Later, he sailed around the world in his boat, becoming the first person ever to do so in a boat of that size. The voyage took him three years to complete.[257]

**The Tilikum at the turn of the century
Galiano Archives MOR69**

Spotlight Cove, on the northwest side of Galiano, provides for a long beach. The trail to the beach is accessible by way of Porlier Pass Road. (#3 on the map)

Twiss Road Beach

The beach off Twiss Road, on the southeast side of Galiano, is dotted with driftwood. It provides for views of Gossip Island to the east. (#15 on the map)

Galiano Island

Whaler Bay

In the 1880's, a settler moved from Retreat Cove to a bay. There, he built a log cabin and started a family.[258] Unfortunately, a few years later, his wife passed away.[259]

When his sister emigrated from Ireland to help him raise his two baby sons, he decided to built a larger home.[260]

The settler's new home had three large rooms on the main floor and three bedrooms upstairs, all of which were plastered on the inside. At one end of a long verandah, there was a milk-cooling room. At the other end, was a summer kitchen with an adjacent wood shed.[261]

Upon completion of the house, the settler's sister married and moved off the Island, leaving him with a large home to maintain.[262]

Desperate, the settler hired a housekeeper, who managed his home and family well. Over time, he made her his second wife. Ironically, she died in childbirth shortly after the turn of the century.[263]

At the onset of World War I, the settler drowned while crossing from Mayne Island to Pender Island in his boat.[264]

Whaler Bay is a lovely bay on the southeast side of Galiano. Once an anchorage for small whaling boats,[265] it is now used as a home for commercial fishing boats. The coves around the shores of the bay provide for good anchorages.

Wildlife to Observe

When the first settlers arrived in the southern Gulf Islands, they found a perfect sanctuary for wildlife. Wild pigs rooted in the marshes, elk stalked the hills and the small black bear foraged among the fruit shrubs. The hunting cry of the gray wolf and the scream of the cougar were frequent sounds.

An early cougar hunter
Salt Spring Archives 989024027

Although there are no large predators in the Gulf Islands today, the wildlife is still very diverse. The Islands are a great place to watch wildlife and are most spectacular in the spring. However, although, many species are commonly seen throughout the year, some are more elusive and it requires a bit of luck to spot them.

Some plant and animal specifies found in the Gulf Islands cannot be found anywhere else in Canada. The rarely seen Sharp-Tailed Snake is known to exist only in the Gulf Islands and on the southeastern portion of Vancouver Island.

There are some interesting species of wildlife that are rare and endangered. However, only the most commonly seen species of wildlife have been listed in this book.

Marine Mammals

Marine mammals have adapted characteristics to survive and prosper in environments that are hostile to most land mammals. Some migrate from the southern Gulf Islands to tropical habitats that are suitable for birthing.

Northern migrations begin early in the spring and southern migrations begin in the fall. Many marine mammals can frequently be seen swimming through Active Pass.

Galiano Island

Orca Pass
International Stewardship Area

The Orca Pass initiative is a citizen-led project whereby both Canada and the United States have agreed to cooperate on the preservation and protection of the Orca Pass International Stewardship Area. This area is a delicate marine mammal and sea-life environment around the southern Gulf Islands.

Harbour Porpoises, or Common Porpoises, are small whales that only grow to 1.8 m in length. They are brown to black in color, with a white underside. They can frequently be seen swimming through Active Pass.

Harbour Seals, also known as Common Seals or Leopard Seals, can grow to 1.8 m in length. They are gray with a unique pattern of fine, dark spots.

They have a whiskery nose and bulging eyes. Their hind flippers extend backwards.

There was a Canadian bounty on Harbour Seals for several decades after the turn of the century. However, today, they can be found in quiet, rocky places where they can land during low tide.

Seals are the marine mammals you are most likely to see around the southern Gulf Islands, but they will dive into the water if they are approached too closely.

Orcas, also known as Killer Whales, Black Fish or Grampus, are actually dolphins. They are black with a white chest and sides. They sport a white patch above and behind the eye. They can grow to 9.5 m in length and weigh as much as 10,000 kilograms.

Galiano Island

The coast of British Columbia is well known as the place on *Elehe* (Earth) to watch migrating and resident whales feeding and breaching.

Resident whales are almost exclusively fish eaters. However, transient whales eat harbour seals, sea lion pups, birds, and even porpoises and dolphins if they can catch them.

At the time of this writing, there were 81 resident whales in the southern Gulf Islands, as well as the San Juan Islands and Washington State. They are usually seen in pods of 5-25 animals.

Pacific White-Sided Dolphin are greenish-black with a white belly and grey stripes along their sides. They can grow to a length of 2.5 m. Large groups of dolphin readily approach boats in Active Pass in the spring and fall. Fishermen often refer to them as 'lags'.

Sea Lions can grow to 3 m in length and weigh up to 1,000 kg. They are brown to black in color. Some species

were put on the U.S. endangered species list and have since been the object of intense study. Some species are intelligent and adaptable, and are often trained as entertainers at ocean parks and zoos.

Around the southern Gulf Islands, sea lions delight in throwing kelp around and body surfing the waves. They can also be seen at the west end of Active Pass, either in the water or hauled up on the rocks around Georgeson Bay.

Otters are reddish-brown to black in color. They are intelligent and very playful, frequently floating and swimming on their backs.

Otters became extinct in British Columbia in the 1920's. In the 1960's, 89 otters were reintroduced from Alaska and have begun to spread again, along the west coast of Vancouver Island.

GaLiaNo ISLaNd

Clams, or Macoma, can live for 20 years or more. Although the Smooth Washington Clam is the mainstay of the clam business, there are several varieties around the southern Gulf Islands, most of which are white in color.

Sea LiFe

The ocean environment around the southern Gulf Islands supports a delicate, yet complex web of life. When the tide recedes, the depressions that retain water between the rocks are called *tidal pools*, which are natural aquariums for an abundance of vertebrates and invertebrates. *Siwash loggers* (beachcombers) can see this life when the tide goes out.

For those who want to gather filter-feeding shellfish from around the southern Gulf Islands, a permit is required to dig and quantities are limited.

If you find a clam shell on the beach surface, the clam is no longer living in it. However, finding live *luk'-ut-chee* (clams) is not difficult if you look in mixed mud, rock and sand. The smallest clams, called *Little-Necks*, can be found just beneath the surface. The larger *Butter Clams*, which can live for 20 years, can be found about 20 cm from the surface. The largest and longest-living clams, called *Horse Clams*, can be found about 30 cm from the surface.

Clams feed, breathe and expel waste through tubes that extend up to the surface of the beach. You can tell if there are clams embedded in a beach if you see water squirting out of the sand. A good place to find clams is on Shell Beach. A small shovel or hand rake works well to uncover them.

Crabs are reddish-brown to purple in color. Some species of crab can grow to a width of 23 cm and can live for 6 years.

You need a trap to actually land crabs that are large enough to eat and catching crabs is a secret kept by *island crabbers* (Gulf Islanders who catch crab).

Because they prefer a sand or mud ocean bottom, you can see small specimens in shallow waters. In fact,

most of the movement you see in tidal pools are crabs scurrying about.

Cockles look somewhat like clams. They are cream-colored with a grey or brown mottled pattern. They have deeply set ridges, which make them easy to identify.

Cockles can often be found on or near the surface of muddy or sandy beaches. Some species can live for up to 16 years.

Jellyfish are not actually fish. They are a member of the invertebrate family. They feed on small fish and zooplankton that become caught in their tentacles where their stinging cells latch onto them. They are usually found floating near the surface of the water or stranded on the beach.

Limpets have an elliptical shell that rises to a peak. Unlike mussels, clams and oysters, limpets have only one shell half, which is usually greenish brown with cream lines radiating down from the peak. The underside has a brown spot in the center.

Limpets can be found attached to the sides of the rocks along the shoreline on the beach.

Mussels found in the southern Gulf Islands are generally dark blue with hints of brown. They can grow to 20 cm in length. They attach themselves to rocks and to wood, especially to pilings.

To gather *to'-luks* (mussels), just locate a colony and pry them loose. As you gather them, make sure the shells are closed tightly or that they snap shut when you grab them.

Oysters are greyish-white in color. Their shells are wavy and mold to the object they attach themselves to. They can grow to 30 cm in length. The Japanese introduced some of the oysters to the southern Gulf Islands, in the 1920's.

The *klógh-klogh* (oyster) can be found attached to rocks on the beach surface. To gather them, you must pry them loose with a sharp tool. If you harvest a supply of oysters, consider leaving the shells on the beach for new generations of oysters.

Galiano Island

Sea Stars, or Starfish, are usually purple in color, but can also be a bright coral color. They can grow to over 36 cm in diameter. The Sea Stars around the southern Gulf Islands are carnivores that feed on mussels and barnacles. They flip their stomach out through their mouth and digest their prey from the inside out.

It is not uncommon to see a Sea Star with a partially regenerated limb. If they lose a limb, they can regenerate it.[266] One of the best places to find Sea Stars is in Dionisio Point Park at low tide.

Snails have long, cylindrical-shaped shells that are gray to brown in color. The shell often has a stripe winding around it. They only grow to 3 cm, but they can live for 10 years. You can find them in shallow water. The Japanese accidentally introduced some species of snails to the Gulf Islands, in the 1920's.

Land Mammals

Hunting is no longer permitted in the Gulf Islands, except by bow and arrow. Because of that, the land mammals that live there are relatively tame.

Columbia Blacktail Deer, or Mowich, are a small sub-species of mule deer. They are the largest land mammals you are likely to see in the southern Gulf Islands.

A major difference between the Columbian Blacktail and other deer is in the way they can leap, and then land with all four legs hitting the ground at the same time. This enables them to change direction in one bound.

You can identify the seasons by the development of a buck's antlers. In the spring, the buds appear on his head. In summer, he grows lush velvet, which coats the antlers. In the fall, the velvet falls off, hardening the antler bone underneath. In winter, the antlers are cast off.

Unfortunately, as cute as they are, deer eliminate the forest understory in their search for food and are widespread enough to support the outer Gulf Islands' fence builders. You can find them just about everywhere.

Douglas Squirrels, or Chickaree, are brown rodents with a bushy tail and a distinctive call. They make their home in tree cavities or in nests constructed of twigs, needles and bark. You can see them leaping from branch to branch in the dense forests around the southern Gulf Islands.

Raccoons have soft, dense, grey fur and a black mask across their face.

They have long tails that are characterized by a pattern of rings. You can see raccoons along some of the beaches around the southern Gulf Islands. Their presence is revealed by human-like handprints, which can be seen in the mud.

Townsend's Chipmunks are brown rodents with black stripes. They hibernate during the winter months. However, in the summer, because they seldom climb trees, they can be seen scurrying along the ground in the dense forests around the southern Gulf Islands.

Birds

The southern Gulf Islands are well known for their bird watching opportunities. The rocky shores are stopover sites for migratory birds and nesting sites for many sea birds.

Over 130 species of marine birds from 22 countries breed, migrate and/or spend the winter in the Strait. Because the climate invites them to reside or visit, the southern Gulf Islands become a *kalakala* (bird) watchers' paradise in the winter. Laughlin Lake, in the Pebble Beach Reserve, is home to at least 55 specifies of resident and migratory birds.

Bald Eagles have a white head and tail, and a contrasting brown body. They can grow to 90 cm tall with a wingspan of 2 m. Although they are indigenous to North America, they were on the brink of extinction late in the 20th century. Fortunately, they have largely recovered and, today, 25 percent of the world's eagle nesting population is found in British Columbia.

Eagles are birds of prey. Their main food supply is the Glaucous-Winged Gull. In the summer, they search for surface-feeding fish, snatching food with aerial acrobatics. They are also good at forcing other birds to drop their prey and will often steal prey from an Osprey.

'Baldies' are commonly seen around the southern Gulf Islands, especially in the spring when they are rearing their young. Those that are old enough to nest often return to the area in which they were raised. Their nests, which are protected by law, can span 3 m across and weigh 900 kg. They eventually collapse under their own weight.

Because they prefer nest sites with a view, you can see them in Montague Harbour Park and Dionisio Point Park, as well as beneath the cliffs in Bodega Ridge Park.

Belted Kingfishers have deep blue or bluish-gray plumage with white markings. The blue feathers on their heads make their heads appear larger than they are. They have a broad, white collar around their neck and a blue band around their chest. The female has an orange band, as well. As loners, they only tolerate one another at mating time.

The Belted Kingfisher is the only species of kingfisher found in the Pacific Northwest. Whenever there is good fishing around the southern Gulf Islands, you can expect to find them perched on trees or posts, close to the water. They are a noisy bird with a loud, rattling call. On a calm winter day, the kingfisher's call can often be heard in Montague Harbour Park.

Brown Creepers have a mottled brown coloration and long, stiff tail-feathers. Their cheerful song has been described as 'trees, trees, trees, see the trees'.

Brown Creepers are common, year-round residents of the forests on the Islands. A creeper will typically forage upwards on tree bark. As it nears the treetop, it drops to the base of a nearby tree to begin its ascent all over again. If it is frightened, it will flatten itself against the tree trunk, becoming almost impossible to see.

Canada Geese have a black head and neck. They have a broad, white chin strap with a contrasting brown body. In flight, they slice through the skies in 'V-formations' or in long lines.

Canada Geese mate for life and are faithful to their breeding grounds, returning to their birth sites each spring.

They are abundant waterfowl that can be found year-round.

Cormorants are dark, long-necked, diving birds with long bills. They often stand upright and hold their wings out to dry. They can be seen flying in single file, floating low in the water, or hanging out on rocks or pilings in a bay.

Great Blue Herons, also known as a Shagpoke or Shikspoke, are long-legged, greyish-blue, wading birds. They can grow to 1.2 m tall with a 2 m wingspan. They have a plume of black feathers behind their eye.

Great Blue Herons can be seen standing like sentinels, gazing into the water at low tide, in search of food. They feed in shallow water and spear fish or frogs with their long, sharp bills. They will also raid goldfish ponds in Islanders' backyards. You can hear them croak as they fly laboriously to their enormous nests of sticks.

The herons found in the southern Gulf Islands are a distinctive subspecies. They are year-round residents. You can find them in Montague Harbour Park.

Grouse generally have a brown camouflage pattern. Some species are so well camouflaged that they allow humans, and even predators, to approach very closely. Grouse are year-round, ground-dwelling residents of the Islands' forests. First Nations used to boil them in a soup.

Gulls are graceful in flight, voracious when feeding and capable of many sounds. One small, delicate species is most often seen around the southern Gulf Islands in winter. However, other species can be found, year-round.

Ospreys are mostly white underneath, with contrasting dark coloration above. They display a dark line through their eye. Most Ospreys depart the southern Gulf Islands in the fall and return in the spring.

Ospreys are aggressors and birds of prey. An Osprey will attack an eagle if it comes too close to its nest.

When an Osprey sees a fish in the water, it will suddenly tuck in its wings and plummet down, throwing its feet forward at the last minute. It will then grasp the fish with its talons and carry it with its head forward, to cut down on wind resistance. For this reason, some people refer to them as 'fish hawks'.

Pacific Loons are dark brown with a white belly. In winter, they display a border between the front and the back of their neck. This changes in the summer when they display a velvety grey head, a dark throat and a checkered back.

Loons are diving birds, preferring areas of *skookumchuck* (strong currents), where they dive for fish. Sometimes, in the spring, hundreds of them can be seen diving in Active Pass. In summer, they display a velvety grey head, a dark throat and a checkered back.

In winter, Pacific Loons display a border between the front and the back of their neck. Some of North America's largest wintering population exists in the southern Gulf Islands. They arrive in the fall from their northern breeding grounds.

Red-Breasted Nuthatches are small, short-tailed birds with sharp beaks. They have a black cap with a white eye-stripe and a bit of rusty coloring on their chest. When they are building a nest, their hammering can sound like that of a woodpecker.

Unlike the Brown Creeper, nuthatches spiral down tree trunks, headfirst, pulling insects out of the bark. They will stay close to home year-round if there is enough food or a bird feeder in the area. They can be found in the mature, cone-bearing forests around the southern Gulf Islands, where their call is a familiar sound.

Red-Tailed Hawks have broad wings and a broad, rust-colored tail. They are designed for soaring on thermals of warm, rising air. They are birds of prey and will eat almost any small animal. The blood-curdling scream of a Red-Tailed Hawk is what is often heard in the movies. They can be found virtually everywhere in the southern Gulf Islands, year-round.

Rufous Hummingbirds can fly left, right, up, down, backwards and even upside down. When hovering, they hold their bodies upright and flap their wings horizontally in a 'figure eight'. Most 'hummers' flap their wings 12,000 times per minute, which is why they are seen as a blur.

Rufous Hummingbirds must eat half their weight in sugar each day. In early spring, they leave their wintering grounds in Mexico and make their way north, flower-by-flower, sucking the nectar from the bloom of the Red-Flowering Currant and Salmonberry shrubs. A long, stiletto bill assists them in this lifestyle. They can be found in the Islands' forests and gardens.

Steller's Jays are the avian emblem of British Columbia. They are deep bluish-black in color and are frequently mistaken for the eastern Blue Jay. They have a dark crest that raises and lowers to indicate their state of agitation.

Announcing their arrival with a raucous call, Steller's Jays will descend upon a bird feeder, scattering smaller birds from it. As year-round residents that live on the Islands' forest slopes, they also like to grab acorns from trees, such as Garry Oak.

Swallows winter in South America and are seen in the southern Gulf Islands in the summer. Several varieties exist, ranging in color from blue to green to brown to purple.

In the last half of the 20th century, the population of Western Purple Martins, the largest species in the swallow family, has declined drastically.

Since the 1980's, the Georgia Basin Ecological Assessment and Restoration Society has helped the population recover by installing more than 1,100 nest boxes throughout the Strait. Young Purple Martins see the nest boxes and return to them each spring.[267]

Turkey Vultures have two-toned wings and a naked, red head. They are birds of prey that are usually seen in flight with wings in a 'V-formation'.

Their tilting flight is an energy-saving strategy. Without turning it's head, a Turkey Vulture can see views of the land below. It will spiral upwards within a thermal of warm, rising air, then descend in a long glide to catch the next thermal.

In the fall, Turkey Vultures use the southern Gulf Islands as stepping stones as they head south to California and Mexico. One of the best places to find them is perched in the trees in Bodega Ridge Park.

PLaceS to FiSH

Gulf Island waters are renowned throughout North America for their salmon, bottom fish and shellfish.

Active Pass is a prized salmon-fishing ground, providing the best summer fishing in the Gulf Islands and salmon fishing in the Georgia Strait is a year-round sport, with the best fishing occurring in winter.

Galiano Island

Active Pass is famous for some of the greatest Spring and Coho salmon fishing in the world. It is a crossroads for salmon returning to spawn in the Fraser River, which has the world's largest, natural, salmon runs.

Keep in mind that the excellent fishing occurs in the Pass during months when the ferry traffic is at its highest, and accidents between ferries and sport fishermen have occurred there.

Porlier Pass, off the north end of Galiano, is also known for its salmon fishing. However, tides in Porlier Pass run up to 9 knots and are dangerous to small boats.

Some of the finest salmon fishing in the Gulf Islands is off East Point, on the east side on Saturna Island. It is fished throughout the summer by anglers from both sides of Georgia Strait.

Home to sea-run Cutthroat Trout, Chum and Coho Salmon, Lyall Creek, on Saturna Island, has unusually high numbers of fish for the region and provides for good fishing off the mouth of Lyall Harbour.

You can also fish for salmon off the rocks at Bellhouse Provincial Park, on Galiano Island, and between St. John Point and Conconi Reef, on Mayne Island.

If the salmon fishing is slow, you can try fishing for other bottom fish, such as Ling Cod, Red Snapper, Black Bass and Sole.

Sporades Tours

Sporades Tours provides for fishing charters in the Gulf Islands. It is based on Galiano. Phone: 1-877-588 3506

Galiano Island

Creatures to Cook

In the gold-mining camps of the late 1800's, an expensive egg omelet, called the *Hangtown Fry*, was prepared for hungry gold miners. It contained fried breaded oysters and bacon.[268]

Early settlers eating a meal, 1930's
Salt Spring Archives 1994137079

Today, seafood is incredibly easy to prepare. With a little basic knowledge, you can become an expert in no time at all. The most important thing to remember when cooking seafood is not to overcook it. It is also very important to pay strict attention to the health advisories, as paralytic shellfish poisoning is potentially deadly.

FISH

The freshness and flavor of a fish, such as salmon, cod and sole, can be preserved all day by killing it immediately and keeping it cool. To clean the fish, simply slice it lengthwise and remove the gills, as well as the contents of the carcass. Then, wash the fish before wrapping it in paper.

After the fish has been cleaned, cut through the backbone so you can *butterfly it* (spread the two sides down) on a grill or frying pan. Simmer the fish over low heat until the bones can be pulled away from the meat.

Crab

A crab should be kept alive until it is time to cook it. Before you cook a crab, first remove its shell. To remove the shell, point the crab away from your body, and grasp its legs and pinchers with your hands facing up. Hit it against a hard surface so the top of its shell lifts off.

Then, simply break the crab in half and discard the contents of the carcass. To cook the carcass, just boil it and serve it with melted butter for dipping.

CLaMS aNd MuSSeLS

To cook clams or mussels, just drop them into a pot of boiling water and leave them until their shells open. Discard the green substance from the shells of the clams. Once they have been removed from their shells, you can fry them in butter, or cook them in a pot with bacon, potatoes and milk.

OySters

It is best to *shuck* (open) oysters right on the beach and leave the shells there for new generations of oysters. Shucked oysters can then be fried with Worcestershire sauce or added to a chowder. They can even be eaten raw.

If you prefer to cook your oysters, just throw them on hot coals with the cupped half of the shell up and leave them until their shells open.

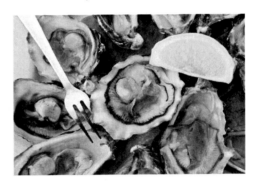

FLora to Appreciate

For most early settlers, timber was an obstruction to destroy, rather than a resource to utilize. When the first settlers began to clear their Island homesteads, they slashed and burned much of the timber they felled.[269]

Many settlers soon supplemented their income by logging, using their horses and oxen to drag logs along skid roads.[270]

At the turn of the century, a building boom boosted the logging industry. Over the next six years, it grew by over 30 percent, making up 40 percent of British Columbia's economy.[271]

GaLiaNo ISLaNd

Early settlers falling a tree, 1930's
Salt Spring Archives 1994137078

Today, the unique environment in the Gulf Islands is host to a wide diversity of plant life. The flora is probably the most varied in all of British Columbia.

The southern Gulf Islands sits in one of the smallest climate zones in the west. In this zone, the rain shadow holds rainfall to less than 75 cm annually. The climate zone is noted for over 250 beautiful, spring, wild flowers - too many to list in this little book.

Trees

The southern Gulf Islands are part of the coastal, Douglas-Fir, plant community, which is marked by the predominance of Douglas-Fir, Arbutus and Garry Oak trees. Its very limited range includes only the southern Gulf Islands, Washington State and part of Vancouver Island.

Amabilis means *lovely*. The Amabilis Fir, or Silver Fir, is a tall, straight tree that can grow to 55 m in height. It has flat needles that are dark and shiny, with white lines underneath.

Arbutus, or Madrona, are Canada's only native, broad-leaved evergreen and exist on only a very small portion of the extreme West Coast. They are indigenous to the southern Gulf Islands.

The unusual Arbutus tree produces bright red berries. It sheds its thin, smooth, cinnamon-colored bark. Although they are deciduous, Arbutus do not drop their leaves in the winter.

First Nations believe that the survivors of the *Great Flood* used the Arbutus tree to anchor their canoe to the top of Mount Newton on Vancouver Island.

Today, you can find fine examples of Arbutus in Matthews Point Park, around Coon Bay and around the Galiano Island Cemetery.

Bitter Cherry is a small tree that produces pinkish flowers. The flowers develop into bright red, bitter cherries. First Nations peeled off the stringy bark of the Bitter Cherry for wrapping harpoon and arrow joints.

Black Cottonwood is a hardy tree with a straight trunk. It can grow to 50 m tall. It has large, sticky, fragrant buds. The Black Cottonwood is named for the white hairs on its seeds, which float through the air like wisps of cotton.

First Nations made canoes from cottonwood trees. Some tribes produced soap from the inner bark. The Hudson's Bay Company reportedly continued using this method in their own brand of soaps.

Black Hawthorn is a small tree that produces white flowers. The flowers develop into small, edible, blackish-purple fruits that are shaped like apples. The thorns of the Black Hawthorn were used by First Nations as game pieces when playing games.

Broadleaf Maple, or Bigleaf Maple, is the largest maple tree in Canada, reaching heights of 36 m. Its leaves measure up to 30 cm across. It is restricted to the southwest corner of British Columbia.

First Nations called the Broadleaf Maple the *Paddle Tree* because they made paddles out of the wood.

Cascara is a small tree that produces small, greenish-yellow flowers that develop into bluish-black berries. First Nations boiled the bark of the cascara into a tea that was drank as a strong laxative.

Douglas-Fir, also known as the Oregon Pine or Nootka Pine, is the dominant species of tree in the southern Gulf Islands. It can be found just about everywhere. It can grow to 85 m high and 2 m wide. Its bark is very thick and deeply grooved.

First Nations had many uses for Douglas-Fir. They used it to make fish hooks and handles. They used the wood and boughs as fuel for cooking. Its boughs were frequently used for covering the floors of lodges.

Today, you can find wonderful examples of Douglas-Fir at the Pebble Beach Reserve, in Bodega Ridge Park and Matthews Point Park, and around the Galiano Cemetery.

GALIANO ISLAND

The Grand Fir is also found in the southern Gulf Islands. It is easily distinguished from other fir trees by its flat needle sprays that grow in two rows.

Garry Oaks, or Oregon White Oaks, are picturesque, gnarled, hardwood trees. They can grow to 20 m in height and can live for up to 500 years. Oaks have thick, grooved, greyish-black bark. They produce small acorns with a scaly cup on one end.

In Canada, Garry Oak are found almost exclusively on the southeastern portion of Vancouver Island, and in the southern Gulf Islands. Unfortunately, their numbers are in decline throughout the range.

Typically, the Garry Oak forms open parkland and meadows. However, from the time the southern Gulf Islands were first settled until the 1950's, much of the land that contained the oak was either logged or converted to farms. Since cone-bearing trees grow faster than

Garry Oak. This creates shade where the oak cannot regenerate.

Although you can find small examples of Garry Oak in the southern Gulf Islands today, less than five percent of the original Garry Oak habitat remains. Some of the best places to see Garry Oak is in Bodega Ridge Provincial Park and Matthews Point Park, and around Coon Bay.

Galiano Island

Lodgepole Pine trees are commonly cut down for Christmas trees. They can grow to 40 m in height. Their cones often remain closed for years and open from the heat of a fire. This allows them to develop rapidly after a forest fire.

The Western White Pine is also found in the southern Gulf Islands. It is a symmetrical tree that can grow to 40 m in height, or taller. It is a five-needle pine. First Nations called it the *Dancing Tree*. They boiled its bark into a tea, which they drank to treat tuberculosis and rheumatism.

In the early 1900's, a shipment of Eastern White Pine was imported to the mainland from France. It carried a fungus called White Pine Blister Rust, which kills young Western White Pine trees. The fungus spread to the southern Gulf Islands so quickly that, by the 1920's, it was established throughout most of the tree range.[272]

Pacific Crabapple trees produce pinkish, fragrant, apple blossoms. The blossoms develop into small, reddish apples that are somewhat tart. During preservation, the apples become sweeter.

Pacific Dogwood is an irregular tree that produces white flowers with purple tips. The flowers develop into clusters of bright red berries. The blossom of the dogwood is the floral emblem of British Columbia.

Pacific Dogwood is one of the few plants protected by law in British Columbia. However, in spite of its protection, it has often been illegally cut down.

Pacific Willow are tall, slender trees with pale yellow leaves associated with a flower. Although they only grow to 12 m tall, they are one of the largest native willows on the West Coast.

Red Alder is an aggressive, fast-growing hardwood tree that does not live much past 50 years. The wood of the alder provides one of the best fuels for smoking fish.

Sitka Spruce, or Airplane Spruce, are large trees that commonly grow to 70 m tall and 2 m across. First Nations fashioned watertight hats and baskets from the roots, which also provided materials for ropes and fishing line.

Western Hemlock is a large tree that can grow to 50 m tall. It has sweeping branches and feathery foliage. Unfortunately, its shallow rooting system makes it susceptible to being blown over

GaLiaNo ISLaNd

by wind. Because its wood is very easy to work with, some First Nations carved it into dishes.

Mountain Hemlock also grows in the southern Gulf Islands. It has drooping branches that have an upward sweep at the tip. In dense forests, its needles form flat sprays.

Western Red Cedar, or Canoe Cedar, is British Columbia's official tree. It is very aromatic and has graceful, swooping branches. The cedar can grow to 60 m tall and its trunk spreads widely at its base.

The cedar was considered the *Tree Of Life* by the First Nations who used its wood for dugout canoes, boxes, tools and paddles. From the inner bark, they made rope, clothing, and baskets. Most of their dwellings were constructed of large boards split from cedar logs.

Western Red Cedars live a long life, sometimes to over 1,000 years. As a result, they can be found just about everywhere in the southern Gulf Islands. One of the best places to find them on Galiano is in Bluffs Park.

The Yellow-Cedar is also found in the southern Gulf Islands. It is the oldest tree in the area. Some are 1,500 years old. However, unlike the Western Red Cedar, the crushed leaves of the Yellow-Cedar smell like mildew.

Western Yew, or Pacific Yew, is a small evergreen tree that has reddish, papery bark. Its trunk is often twisted and fluted. Although the yew is a cone-bearing tree, it produces a single seed. A bright red, fleshy cup, which looks like a large berry, surrounds the seed. Beware of the seed, as it is poisonous.

The tough wood of the Western Yew was highly prized by First Nations. Because it displays a polished surface, it was used for carving.

Shrubs and Ferns

A characteristic feature of the shrubs in the southern Gulf Islands is the variety and abundance that exist in the Heather family. These shrubs dominate the understory of the Islands' mature forests, as well as in non-forested habitats. Many of the shrubs give way to edible *olali* (berries). First Nations ate these berries raw or boiled into cakes.

Black Raspberry, or Blackcap, is an erect shrub that has stems with curved prickles. It produces pinkish flowers that develop into hairy, purplish-black berries that are very tasty.

Black Twinberry, or Bearberry Honeysuckle, is an erect to straggly shrub. It produces yellow, tubular flowers, which develop into pairs of shiny, black, inedible berries.

Bog Cranberry is a dwarf shrub that only grows to 40 cm tall. It produces deep pink flowers that have petals that bend backwards. Its berries are pale pink to dark red in color.

Bracken Fern has a stout stem with a feathery frond. Its fronds were used by First Nations as a protective layer in food storage containers, on berry-drying racks and in pit ovens.

Copperbush is a leafy shrub with loose, shredding, copper-colored bark. Its flowers are also copper-colored. Its fruit develop as round capsules. It is one of only a few of the plants in its classification found exclusively in Western North America.

Devil's Club is an erect to sprawling shrub. It has thick, crooked stems that are often entangled and armed with numerous, large, yellowish spines. The wood of the shrub has a sweet smell. Its leaves are shaped like that of a maple leaf and it produces white flowers.

Related to the Ginseng plant, Devil's Club is one of the most important of all medicinal plants. Sticks made from Devil's Club were used by First Nations as protective charms. When burned, the charcoal from this shrub was used to make face paint for dancers and for tattoo ink.

Dull Oregon Grape is a common, low-growing evergreen shrub with leaves that resemble that of holly. Bright yellow flowers appear in the spring, followed by dark purple, edible berries in the summer. The berries make great jelly. Tall Oregon Grape is another shrub that can be found in the southern Gulf Islands, but in drier areas.

Evergreen Huckleberry has branches that bear leathery leaves lined with sharp teeth. Its clusters of pink flowers produce black berries with a flavor similar to that of a blueberry. Black Mountain Huckleberry is also found in the southern Gulf Islands. It thrives in old burned sites that have only sparse tree regeneration.

False Azalea, or False Huckleberry, is an erect to straggly, spreading shrub, which resembles both the Azalea plant, as well as huckleberry plants. It produces pink to yellow flowers, which develop into inedible fruit. The leaves turn a bright crimson color in the fall.

False Box is a low, dense, evergreen shrub that resembles the Kinnikinnick plant. It produces tiny, maroon colored flowers that have a pleasant fragrance. It has reddish-brown branches that are often used in floral arrangements.

Goats' Beard, or Spaghetti Flower, is a robust rose bush. It produces white flower clusters that resemble goats' beards. First Nations used the roots for medicinal purposes.

Gummy Gooseberry is an erect to spreading shrub with sticky leaves. It produces reddish colored flowers in drooping clusters. Its flowers, which produce nectar that is eaten by hummingbirds, develop into dark purple, hairy berries. The Wild Gooseberry, which produces green or purple flowers, can also be found in the southern Gulf Islands.

Gorse is a non-native shrub with vicious spines that can form impenetrable thickets. Unlike most plants that grow poorly in soils low in nitrogen, it can remove nitrogen from the air. This enables it to thrive in soils that are low in nitrogen. Gorse is a fire hazard.

Hairy Manzanita is an erect or spreading evergreen with very hairy leaves. Its branches have reddish-brown bark that peels. It produces pinkish flowers in hairy clusters. Manzanita means *little apples*, which describes its edible, coffee colored berries. A good place to spot the Hairy Manzanita shrub is in Bodega Ridge Park.

Hardhack, or Steeplebush, is an erect, leggy shrub with many woolly branches. It produces rose colored flowers in a long, narrow cluster. Its fruit develop as clusters of numerous, small, pod-like follicles.

Himalayan Blackberry is an immigrant species from India, which was brought to North America in the 1880's. It has sharp, curved spines that make this precursor of barbed wire a plant to be treated with respect. Gulf Islanders pull

the deadly branches towards them using a straightened coat hanger.

Himalayan Blackberry produces fine white or pink flowers. The fruit, which is a favorite among berry pickers, is easily mistaken for a raspberry. However, unlike the blackberry, the fruit of the raspberry is hollow when picked.

The Himalayan Blackberry grows in abundance in the southern Gulf Islands.

Indian-Plum, or Osoberry, is a tall shrub with purplish-brown bark. It is one

GaLiaNo ISLaNd

of the first plants to flower in the spring, at which time it produces greenish-white flowers in long clusters. Its flowers, which have an unusual scent, are produced before its leaves appear. Its fruit, which is often referred to as *choke-cherries*, resembles small plums.

Kinnikinnick, or Common Bearberry, is a creeping, evergreen, ground cover that forms dense mats. It has small, pinkish flowers. The flowers produce bright red, berries that resemble miniature apples.

Mock Orange is an erect shrub with peeling bark. It produces broad, white, fragrant flowers that develop into oval, woody fruit. First Nations used the wood for making bows and arrows.

Ocean Spray, also called Creambush or Ironwood, is an erect shrub with peeling bark. It produces creamy flowers in dense clusters that resemble lilacs. The flowers remain on the plant over the winter. The strong wood of the shrub was used by First Nations to make knitting needles and other tools.

Orange Honeysuckle, also called Ghost's Swing or Owl's Swing, is a climbing vine that can reach 6 m in height. It produces long, orange, trumpet-shaped flowers with a sweet nectar deep inside. Because they can reach into the flower to suck its nectar, they are a favorite of hummingbirds.

The fruit of the Orange Honeysuckle develop as bunches of translucent,

orange berries. Coastal Indian children also liked to suck the nectar from the base of the honeysuckle flower.

Pacific Ninebark is an erect to spreading shrub with what is believed to be nine layers of peeling bark. It produces small, white flowers that develop into reddish bunches of fruit. First Nations made knitting needles from the wood.

Red Flowering Currant is a tall, erect shrub. It produces white to red flowers in drooping clusters that indicate the beginning of spring. The flowers, which attract hummingbirds, develop into bluish-black berries that are edible, but not very tasty.

Red Elderberry, or Red Elder, is a tall shrub that can grow to 6 m. It produces clusters of creamy flowers with a strong, unpleasant odor. The flowers develop into bright red fruit. Blue Elderberry, which produces blue fruit, can also be found in the southern Gulf Islands.

GaLiaNo ISLaNd

Red-Osier Dogwood is a spreading shrub that can grow to 6 m tall. The branches are often bright red in color. It produces small clusters of greenish flowers, which develop into bluish-white fruit. Although the fruit is very bitter, dogwood is a very important source of food for the deer in the southern Gulf Islands.

Salal means *this plentiful shrub*. This is for good reason, as it is probably the most dominant shrub in the Islands' forests. Salal is an upright or ground crawling plant that can grow sparsely or form a dense barrier that is almost impossible to penetrate. It spreads by suckering layer upon layer.

Salal produces pink flowers that give way to bluish-black berries. The berries, which are juicy, sweet and aromatic, make excellent jams, jellies and wine.

Salmonberry is a branching shrub that often forms dense thickets. It produces pink, red or purple flowers. The flowers develop into mushy, edible, yellow or salmon colored berries. The berries of the Salmonberry are one of the earliest berries to ripen in the spring.

Scotch Broom is a bushy shrub with long, thin stems from which sprout yellow flowers in the spring and pea-shaped pods in the summer.

In the mid-1800's, a European sea captain was immigrating to Vancouver

Island. He brought with him some Scotch Broom seeds that he had picked up from the Hawaiian Islands. Like Gorse, broom can remove the nitrogen it needs from the air, so when the first white settlers began to arrive, it quickly invaded the southern Gulf Islands.[273]

Today, Scotch Broom grows in abundance in the southern Gulf Islands. It produces a toxin that can depress the heart and nervous system. It is also a fire hazard. Gulf Islanders can often be seen participating in a *Broom Bash* (an event where Broom is destroyed).

Sitka Alder is a tall shrub that can grow to 5 m. It produces a spike-like flower cluster. It also produces clusters of cones from which tiny nuts can be shaken.

Sitka Mountain Ash is an erect shrub that produces small, white clusters of flowers. Its red, berry-like fruits are edible, but very bitter.

Stink Currant is an erect shrub with a skunky smell. It produces greenish clusters of flowers that develop into long clusters of edible, bluish-black berries.

Soopolallie, also called Soapberry or Canadian Buffalo-Berry, is a spreading shrub with branches that are covered with scabs. It produces yellowish-brown flowers. Its bright red berries, which feel soapy to the touch, were used by First Nations to make ice cream.

Sword-Fern, also known as the Pala-Pala plant, is one of the most abundant of the ferns found in the southern Gulf Islands. It is often found growing, along with Western Red Cedar, in damp shady forests. Deer Fern, which resembles the Sword-Fern, also grows in the southern Gulf Islands.

White-Flowered Rhododendron is a slender, erect shrub with peeling bark. It produces clusters of creamy, cup-shaped flowers. Rhododendron is often found along with the False Azalea and Copperbush plants.

Galiano Island

Credits

Credits

Historical Photos

British Columbia Archives and Records Services

Royal British Columbia Museum

British Columbia Ferry Services Archives

Salt Spring Archives

Galiano Museum & Archives

Donald New

Current Photos

Dreamstime™
Tony Campbell, David Coleman, Galina Barskaya, Paul Wolf, Scott Pehrson, Marilyn Barbone, Steffen Foerster, Steve Degenhardt, Melissa King, Randy McKown, Kutt Niinepuu, Dennis Sabo, Jason Cheever, Ryan Tacay, Costin Cojocaru, Marilyna Barbone, Nick Stubbs, Francois etienne Du plessis, Pete Setrac, Penny Riches, Dwight Hegel, Tom Hirtreiter, Elena Ray, Norman Pogson, Hannu Liivaar, Patricia Marroquin, Franc Podgorsek, Keith Naylor, Andrew Barker, Elina Gareeva, Richard Gunion, Silas Brown, Jannelle Althoff, Bobby Deal, Yula Zubritsky, Dick Sunderland, Elena Elisseeva, Dan Bannister, Jaimie Duplass, Natthias Nordmeyer, Svetlana Tikhonova, Mark Rasmussen, David Kay, David Pruter

Georgia Strait Alliance
Orca Pass International Stewardship Area

Gulf Islands Water Taxi
Water Taxis

Harbour Air
Beaver Planes

Ken Smith (Galiano Island)
Halloween, Galiano Fiesta, Montague Harbour Marina, Island Time 5 Star B&B, Spanish Longboat, Clowns, Slow Pitch Tournament, Galiano Triathlon

Credits

Acknowledgements

The Gulf Islanders: Sound Heritage, Volume V, Number 4

Island Heritage Buildings – Thomas K. Ovanin, Islands Trust

A Gulf Islands Patchwork: Some Early Events on the Islands of Galiano, Mayne, Saturna, North and South Pender – British Columbia Historical Association

More Tales from the Outer Gulf Islands: An Anthology of Memories and Anecdotes – British Columbia Historical Association

Homesteads and Snug Harbours: The Gulf Islands – Peter Murray

Galiano: Houses And People, Looking back to 1930 – Elizabeth Steward

The Terror Of The Coast: Land Alienation And Colonial War On Vancouver Island And The Gulf Islands – Chris Arnett

Vanishing British Columbia – Michael Kluckner

The Gulf Islands Explorer: The Outdoor Guide – Bruce Obee

Exploring the Best of the Southern Gulf Islands & Sidney: Premier Issue 2005

Hiking the Gulf Islands: An Outdoor Guide to BC's Enchanted Isles – Charles Kahn

Plants of the Pacific Northwest Coast – Pojar and Mackinnon

Birds of the Pacific Northwest Coast – Nancy Baron & John Acorn

Mammals of the Northwest: Washington, Oregon, Idaho and British Columbia – Earl J. Larrison

The Beachcomber's Guide to Seashore Life in the Pacific Northwest– J. Duane Sept

A Year on the Wild Side: - Briony Penn

WetCoast Words: A Dictionary of British Columbia Words and Phrases – Tom Parkin

Notes

[1] **More Tales from the Outer Gulf Islands:** An Anthology of Memories and Anecdotes – British Columbia Historical Association, pp. 209-213

[2] **More Tales from the Outer Gulf Islands:** An Anthology of Memories and Anecdotes – British Columbia Historical Association, pp. 215

[3] **Island Heritage Buildings** – Thomas K. Ovanin, Islands Trust, pp. 98

[4] **More Tales from the Outer Gulf Islands:** An Anthology of Memories and Anecdotes – British Columbia Historical Association, pp. 209-213

[5] **Homesteads and Snug Harbours:** The Gulf Islands – Peter Murray, pp. 41 and **Galiano:** Houses And People, Looking back to 1930 – Elizabeth Steward, pp. 58

[6] **Island Heritage Buildings** – Thomas K. Ovanin, Islands Trust, pp. 98

[7] **More Tales from the Outer Gulf Islands:** An Anthology of Memories and Anecdotes – British Columbia Historical Association, pp. 212

[8] **Mayne Island & The Outer Gulf Islands:** A History – Marie Elliott, pp. 4 & 13

[9] **A Gulf Islands Patchwork:** Some Early Events on the Islands of Galiano, Mayne, Saturna, North and South Pender – British Columbia Historical Association, pp. 19, 131 & 144

[10] **More Tales from the Outer Gulf Islands:** An Anthology of Memories and Anecdotes – British Columbia Historical Association, pp. 265

[11] **More Tales from the Outer Gulf Islands:** An Anthology of Memories and Anecdotes – British Columbia Historical Association, pp. 265

[12] **More Tales from the Outer Gulf Islands:** An Anthology of Memories and Anecdotes – British Columbia Historical Association, pp. 265

[13] **Galiano:** Houses And People, Looking back to 1930 – Elizabeth Steward, pp. 30

[14] **Galiano Island Archives website**

[15] **Mayne Island & The Outer Gulf Islands**: A History – Marie Elliott, pp. 96

[16] **A Gulf Islands Patchwork:** Some Early Events on the Islands of Galiano, Mayne, Saturna, North and South Pender – British Columbia Historical Association, pp. 141

[17] **Galiano:** Houses And People, Looking back to 1930 – Elizabeth Steward, pp. 30 & 133

[18] **Salt Spring:** The Story of an Island – Charles Kahn, pp. 42

[19] **Homesteads and Snug Harbours:** The Gulf Islands – Peter Murray, pp. 34

[20] **A Gulf Islands Patchwork:** Some Early Events on the Islands of Galiano, Mayne, Saturna, North and South Pender – British Columbia Historical Association, pp. 141 and map

[21] **Homesteads and Snug Harbours:** The Gulf Islands – Peter Murray, pp. 41

[22] **A Gulf Islands Patchwork:** Some Early Events on the Islands of Galiano, Mayne, Saturna, North and South Pender – British Columbia Historical Association, pp. 141

[23] **Galiano:** Houses And People, Looking back to 1930 – Elizabeth Steward, pp. 133

Notes

[24] **More Tales from the Outer Gulf Islands:** An Anthology of Memories and Anecdotes – British Columbia Historical Association, pp. 211, 212 & 244

[25] **More Tales from the Outer Gulf Islands:** An Anthology of Memories and Anecdotes – British Columbia Historical Association, pp. 211, 212 & 244 and **Galiano Island Archives website**

[26] **Galiano:** Houses And People, Looking back to 1930 – Elizabeth Steward, pp. 72 and **More Tales from the Outer Gulf Islands:** An Anthology of Memories and Anecdotes – British Columbia Historical Association, pp. 244

[27] **Galiano:** Houses And People, Looking back to 1930 – Elizabeth Steward, pp. 72 and **More Tales from the Outer Gulf Islands:** An Anthology of Memories and Anecdotes – British Columbia Historical Association, pp. 244

[28] **Galiano:** Houses And People, Looking back to 1930 – Elizabeth Steward, pp. 73

[29] **More Tales from the Outer Gulf Islands:** An Anthology of Memories and Anecdotes – British Columbia Historical Association, pp. 244

[30] **More Tales from the Outer Gulf Islands:** An Anthology of Memories and Anecdotes – British Columbia Historical Association, pp. 244

[31] **More Tales from the Outer Gulf Islands:** An Anthology of Memories and Anecdotes – British Columbia Historical Association, pp. 246

[32] **More Tales from the Outer Gulf Islands:** An Anthology of Memories and Anecdotes – British Columbia Historical Association, pp. 246

[33] **Galiano:** Houses And People, Looking back to 1930 – Elizabeth Steward, pp. 30 & 73

[34] **Galiano:** Houses And People, Looking back to 1930 – Elizabeth Steward, pp. 30

[35] **A Gulf Islands Patchwork:** Some Early Events on the Islands of Galiano, Mayne, Saturna, North and South Pender – British Columbia Historical Association, pp. 157

[36] **Homesteads and Snug Harbours:** The Gulf Islands – Peter Murray, pp. 36

[37] **A Gulf Islands Patchwork:** Some Early Events on the Islands of Galiano, Mayne, Saturna, North and South Pender – British Columbia Historical Association, pp. 157

[38] **Galiano:** Houses And People, Looking back to 1930 – Elizabeth Steward, pp. 49

[39] **More Tales from the Outer Gulf Islands:** An Anthology of Memories and Anecdotes – British Columbia Historical Association, pp. 125 & 126

[40] **A Gulf Islands Patchwork:** Some Early Events on the Islands of Galiano, Mayne, Saturna, North and South Pender – British Columbia Historical Association, pp. 102 & 157

[41] **Galiano:** Houses And People, Looking back to 1930 – Elizabeth Steward, pp. 119

[42] **More Tales from the Outer Gulf Islands:** An Anthology of Memories and Anecdotes – British Columbia Historical Association, pp. 215

[43] **Galiano:** Houses And People, Looking back to 1930 – Elizabeth Steward, pp. 50

[44] **Galiano:** Houses And People, Looking back to 1930 – Elizabeth Steward, pp. 50

Notes

[45] **A Gulf Islands Patchwork:** Some Early Events on the Islands of Galiano, Mayne, Saturna, North and South Pender – British Columbia Historical Association, pp. 102 & 157

[46] **Galiano:** Houses And People, Looking back to 1930 – Elizabeth Steward, pp. 119

[47] **Galiano:** Houses And People, Looking back to 1930 – Elizabeth Steward, pp. 50

[48] **Galiano:** Houses And People, Looking back to 1930 – Elizabeth Steward, pp. 50 & 51

[49] **Snapshots of Early Salt Spring and other Favoured Islands:** Mouat's Trading Co. Ltd., pp. 66

[50] **A Gulf Islands Patchwork:** Some Early Events on the Islands of Galiano, Mayne, Saturna, North and South Pender – British Columbia Historical Association, pp. 103

[51] **Island Heritage Buildings** – Thomas K. Ovanin, Islands Trust, pp. 95

[52] **Galiano:** Houses And People, Looking back to 1930 – Elizabeth Steward, pp. 148

[53] **Galiano:** Houses And People, Looking back to 1930 – Elizabeth Steward, pp. 148

[54] **Island Heritage Buildings** – Thomas K. Ovanin, Islands Trust, pp. 95 and **Galiano:** Houses And People, Looking back to 1930 – Elizabeth Steward, pp. 148

[55] **Galiano:** Houses And People, Looking back to 1930 – Elizabeth Steward, pp. 148

[56] **Island Heritage Buildings** – Thomas K. Ovanin, Islands Trust, pp. 95

[57] **More Tales from the Outer Gulf Islands:** An Anthology of Memories and Anecdotes – British Columbia Historical Association, pp. 261-263

[58] **Galiano:** Houses And People, Looking back to 1930 – Elizabeth Steward, pp. 52

[59] **More Tales from the Outer Gulf Islands:** An Anthology of Memories and Anecdotes – British Columbia Historical Association, pp. 124 & 261-263 and **Galiano:** Houses And People, Looking back to 1930 – Elizabeth Steward, pp. 52

[60] **More Tales from the Outer Gulf Islands:** An Anthology of Memories and Anecdotes – British Columbia Historical Association, pp. 124 & 261-263 and **Galiano:** Houses And People, Looking back to 1930 – Elizabeth Steward, pp. 52

[61] **Snapshots of Early Salt Spring and other Favoured Islands:** Mouat's Trading Co. Ltd., pp. 114

[62] **Galiano:** Houses And People, Looking back to 1930 – Elizabeth Steward, pp. 53

[63] **Southern Gulf Islands:** An Altitude SuperGuide – Spalding, Montgomery and Pitt, pp. 50

[64] **Galiano:** Houses And People, Looking back to 1930 – Elizabeth Steward, pp. 30

[65] **Galiano:** Houses And People, Looking back to 1930 – Elizabeth Steward, pp. 56

[66] **A Gulf Islands Patchwork:** Some Early Events on the Islands of Galiano, Mayne, Saturna, North and South Pender – British Columbia Historical Association, pp. 155

[67] **A Gulf Islands Patchwork:** Some Early Events on the Islands of Galiano, Mayne, Saturna, North and South Pender – British Columbia Historical Association, pp. 93 & 155

Notes

[68] **A Gulf Islands Patchwork:** Some Early Events on the Islands of Galiano, Mayne, Saturna, North and South Pender – British Columbia Historical Association, pp. 155

[69] **Galiano:** Houses And People, Looking back to 1930 – Elizabeth Steward, pp. 67

[70] **Galiano:** Houses And People, Looking back to 1930 – Elizabeth Steward, pp. 67

[71] **The Active Page:** Volume 14, Number 12, pp. 12

[72] **Island Tides Newspaper:** Volume 18, Number 3, pp. 8

[73] **Plumper Pass Lockup and Mayne Island Museum** – Mayne Island Agricultural Society, pp. 6

[74] **The Gulf Islands Explorer:** The Complete Guide – Bruce Obee, pp. 143

[75] **More Tales from the Outer Gulf Islands:** An Anthology of Memories and Anecdotes – British Columbia Historical Association, pp. 269-272

[76] **More Tales from the Outer Gulf Islands:** An Anthology of Memories and Anecdotes – British Columbia Historical Association, pp. 269-272

[77] **More Tales from the Outer Gulf Islands:** An Anthology of Memories and Anecdotes – British Columbia Historical Association, pp. 269-272

[78] **More Tales from the Outer Gulf Islands:** An Anthology of Memories and Anecdotes – British Columbia Historical Association, pp. 269-272

[79] **More Tales from the Outer Gulf Islands:** An Anthology of Memories and Anecdotes – British Columbia Historical Association, pp. 269-272

[80] **More Tales from the Outer Gulf Islands:** An Anthology of Memories and Anecdotes – British Columbia Historical Association, pp. 269-272

[81] **More Tales from the Outer Gulf Islands:** An Anthology of Memories and Anecdotes – British Columbia Historical Association, pp. 271 & 272

[82] **More Tales from the Outer Gulf Islands:** An Anthology of Memories and Anecdotes – British Columbia Historical Association, pp. 271 & 272

[83] **Galiano:** Houses And People, Looking back to 1930 – Elizabeth Steward, pp. 56

[84] **The Active Page:** Volume 14, Number 12, pp. 31

[85] **More Tales from the Outer Gulf Islands:** An Anthology of Memories and Anecdotes – British Columbia Historical Association, pp. 227

[86] **More Tales from the Outer Gulf Islands:** An Anthology of Memories and Anecdotes – British Columbia Historical Association, pp. 227

[87] **More Tales from the Outer Gulf Islands:** An Anthology of Memories and Anecdotes – British Columbia Historical Association, pp. 227

[88] **Bellhouse Inn Bed and Breakfast website**

[89] **Hul'qumi'num Treaty Group website**

[90] **Hul'qumi'num Treaty Group website**

[91] **More Tales from the Outer Gulf Islands:** An Anthology of Memories and Anecdotes – British Columbia Historical Association, pp. 278-280 and **Island Heritage Buildings** – Thomas K. Ovanin, Islands Trust, pp. 51

Notes

[92] **More Tales from the Outer Gulf Islands:** An Anthology of Memories and Anecdotes – British Columbia Historical Association, pp. 278-280 and **Island Heritage Buildings** – Thomas K. Ovanin, Islands Trust, pp. 51

[93] **More Tales from the Outer Gulf Islands:** An Anthology of Memories and Anecdotes – British Columbia Historical Association, pp. 278-280 and **Island Heritage Buildings** – Thomas K. Ovanin, Islands Trust, pp. 51

[94] **More Tales from the Outer Gulf Islands:** An Anthology of Memories and Anecdotes – British Columbia Historical Association, pp. 278-280 and **Island Heritage Buildings** – Thomas K. Ovanin, Islands Trust, pp. 51

[95] **More Tales from the Outer Gulf Islands:** An Anthology of Memories and Anecdotes – British Columbia Historical Association, pp. 278-280 and **Island Heritage Buildings** – Thomas K. Ovanin, Islands Trust, pp. 51

[96] **More Tales from the Outer Gulf Islands:** An Anthology of Memories and Anecdotes – British Columbia Historical Association, pp. 278-280 and **Island Heritage Buildings** – Thomas K. Ovanin, Islands Trust, pp. 51

[97] **A Gulf Islands Patchwork:** Some Early Events on the Islands of Galiano, Mayne, Saturna, North and South Pender – British Columbia Historical Association, pp. 91

[98] **Island Heritage Buildings** – Thomas K. Ovanin, Islands Trust, pp. 101

[99] **Bellhouse Inn Bed and Breakfast website**

[100] **Bellhouse Inn Bed and Breakfast website**

[101] **More Tales from the Outer Gulf Islands:** An Anthology of Memories and Anecdotes – British Columbia Historical Association, pp. 275-277

[102] **More Tales from the Outer Gulf Islands:** An Anthology of Memories and Anecdotes – British Columbia Historical Association, pp. 275-277

[103] **Island Heritage Buildings** – Thomas K. Ovanin, Islands Trust, pp. 101

[104] **Island Heritage Buildings** – Thomas K. Ovanin, Islands Trust, pp. 101

[105] **Galiano:** Houses And People, Looking back to 1930 – Elizabeth Steward, pp. 17

[106] **Island Heritage Buildings** – Thomas K. Ovanin, Islands Trust, pp. 101

[107] **Bellhouse Inn Bed and Breakfast website**

[108] **Bellhouse Inn Bed and Breakfast website**

[109] **More Tales from the Outer Gulf Islands:** An Anthology of Memories and Anecdotes – British Columbia Historical Association, pp. 225, 226 & 281

[110] **More Tales from the Outer Gulf Islands:** An Anthology of Memories and Anecdotes – British Columbia Historical Association, pp. 225 & 226

[111] **More Tales from the Outer Gulf Islands:** An Anthology of Memories and Anecdotes – British Columbia Historical Association, pp. 225 & 226

[112] **More Tales from the Outer Gulf Islands:** An Anthology of Memories and Anecdotes – British Columbia Historical Association, pp. 226 & 283

[113] **More Tales from the Outer Gulf Islands:** An Anthology of Memories and Anecdotes – British Columbia Historical Association, pp. 281-286

Notes

[114] **More Tales from the Outer Gulf Islands:** An Anthology of Memories and Anecdotes – British Columbia Historical Association, pp. 281-286

[115] **More Tales from the Outer Gulf Islands:** An Anthology of Memories and Anecdotes – British Columbia Historical Association, pp. 281-286

[116] **Galiano:** Houses And People, Looking back to 1930 – Elizabeth Steward, pp. 22

[117] **Captain`s Quarters website**

[118] **Captain`s Quarters website**

[119] **Captain`s Quarters website**

[120] **Captain`s Quarters website**

[121] **Galiano Museum and Archives:** The Georgeson Collection – Salt Spring Archives

[122] **Galiano Museum and Archives:** The Georgeson Collection – Galiano Archives

[123] **More Tales from the Outer Gulf Islands:** An Anthology of Memories and Anecdotes – British Columbia Historical Association, pp. 207

[124] **Between The Isles:** Life in the Canadian Gulf Islands - Cy Porter, pp. 91

[125] **A Gulf Islands Patchwork:** Some Early Events on the Islands of Galiano, Mayne, Saturna, North and South Pender – British Columbia Historical Association, pp. 102-104

[126] **A Gulf Islands Patchwork:** Some Early Events on the Islands of Galiano, Mayne, Saturna, North and South Pender – British Columbia Historical Association, pp. 95 & 102-104

[127] **Galiano:** Houses And People, Looking back to 1930 – Elizabeth Steward, pp. 36

[128] **A Gulf Islands Patchwork:** Some Early Events on the Islands of Galiano, Mayne, Saturna, North and South Pender – British Columbia Historical Association, pp. 102 & 103

[129] **Galiano:** Houses And People, Looking back to 1930 – Elizabeth Steward, pp. 65

[130] **More Tales from the Outer Gulf Islands:** An Anthology of Memories and Anecdotes – British Columbia Historical Association, pp. 253-256

[131] **A Gulf Islands Patchwork:** Some Early Events on the Islands of Galiano, Mayne, Saturna, North and South Pender – British Columbia Historical Association, pp.102-104

[132] **More Tales from the Outer Gulf Islands:** An Anthology of Memories and Anecdotes – British Columbia Historical Association, pp. 255

[133] **More Tales from the Outer Gulf Islands:** An Anthology of Memories and Anecdotes – British Columbia Historical Association, pp. 253-256

[134] **More Tales from the Outer Gulf Islands:** An Anthology of Memories and Anecdotes – British Columbia Historical Association, pp. 219

[135] **More Tales from the Outer Gulf Islands:** An Anthology of Memories and Anecdotes – British Columbia Historical Association, pp. 234, 257 & 258

[136] **Southern Gulf Islands**: An Altitude SuperGuide – Spalding, Montgomery and Pitt, pp. 51

Notes

[137] **More Tales from the Outer Gulf Islands:** An Anthology of Memories and Anecdotes – British Columbia Historical Association, pp. 234, 257 & 258

[138] **More Tales from the Outer Gulf Islands:** An Anthology of Memories and Anecdotes – British Columbia Historical Association, pp. 257-258

[139] **More Tales from the Outer Gulf Islands:** An Anthology of Memories and Anecdotes – British Columbia Historical Association, pp. 257-258

[140] **Between The Isles:** Life in the Canadian Gulf Islands - Cy Porter, pp. 112

[141] **The Gulf Islanders:** Sound Heritage, Volume V, Number 4, pp. 69

[142] **Galiano:** Houses And People, Looking back to 1930 – Elizabeth Steward, pp. 158

[143] **The Gulf Islanders:** Sound Heritage, Volume V, Number 4, pp. 69 and **Between The Isles:** Life in the Canadian Gulf Islands - Cy Porter, pp. 112

[144] **The Gulf Islanders:** Sound Heritage, Volume V, Number 4, pp. 69 & 70

[145] **The Gulf Islanders:** Sound Heritage, Volume V, Number 4, pp. 69 & 70

[146] **The Gulf Islanders:** Sound Heritage, Volume V, Number 4, pp. 69 & 70

[147] **Island Heritage Buildings** – Thomas K. Ovanin, Islands Trust, pp. 102

[148] **More Tales from the Outer Gulf Islands:** An Anthology of Memories and Anecdotes – British Columbia Historical Association, pp. 225

[149] **Galiano:** Houses And People, Looking back to 1930 – Elizabeth Steward, pp. 2

[150] **Galiano:** Houses And People, Looking back to 1930 – Elizabeth Steward, pp. 168 and **A Gulf Islands Patchwork:** Some Early Events on the Islands of Galiano, Mayne, Saturna, North and South Pender – British Columbia Historical Association, pp. 153

[151] **A Gulf Islands Patchwork:** Some Early Events on the Islands of Galiano, Mayne, Saturna, North and South Pender – British Columbia Historical Association, pp. 153

[152] **Galiano:** Houses And People, Looking back to 1930 – Elizabeth Steward, pp. 168 and **A Gulf Islands Patchwork:** Some Early Events on the Islands of Galiano, Mayne, Saturna, North and South Pender – British Columbia Historical Association, pp. 153

[153] **Galiano:** Houses And People, Looking back to 1930 – Elizabeth Steward, pp. 168

[154] **More Tales from the Outer Gulf Islands:** An Anthology of Memories and Anecdotes – British Columbia Historical Association, pp. 227

[155] **Island Heritage Buildings** – Thomas K. Ovanin, Islands Trust, pp. 102

[156] **More Tales from the Outer Gulf Islands:** An Anthology of Memories and Anecdotes – British Columbia Historical Association, pp. 214-216

[157] **More Tales from the Outer Gulf Islands:** An Anthology of Memories and Anecdotes – British Columbia Historical Association, pp. 214-216 and **A Gulf Islands Patchwork:** Some Early Events on the Islands of Galiano, Mayne, Saturna, North and South Pender – British Columbia Historical Association, pp. 157

[158] **More Tales from the Outer Gulf Islands:** An Anthology of Memories and Anecdotes – British Columbia Historical Association, pp. 214-216

[159] **More Tales from the Outer Gulf Islands:** An Anthology of Memories and Anecdotes – British Columbia Historical Association, pp. 214-216

Notes

[160] **Galiano:** Houses And People, Looking back to 1930 – Elizabeth Steward, pp. 43

[161] **Island Heritage Buildings** – Thomas K. Ovanin, Islands Trust, pp. 99

[162] **Island Heritage Buildings** – Thomas K. Ovanin, Islands Trust, pp. 99

[163] **A Gulf Islands Patchwork:** Some Early Events on the Islands of Galiano, Mayne, Saturna, North and South Pender – British Columbia Historical Association, pp. 88

[164] **A Gulf Islands Patchwork:** Some Early Events on the Islands of Galiano, Mayne, Saturna, North and South Pender – British Columbia Historical Association, pp. 88

[165] **A Gulf Islands Patchwork:** Some Early Events on the Islands of Galiano, Mayne, Saturna, North and South Pender – British Columbia Historical Association, pp. 88

[166] **A Gulf Islands Patchwork:** Some Early Events on the Islands of Galiano, Mayne, Saturna, North and South Pender – British Columbia Historical Association, pp. 88

[167] **A Gulf Islands Patchwork:** Some Early Events on the Islands of Galiano, Mayne, Saturna, North and South Pender – British Columbia Historical Association, pp. 138 and **Galiano Island Archives website**

[168] **A Gulf Islands Patchwork:** Some Early Events on the Islands of Galiano, Mayne, Saturna, North and South Pender – British Columbia Historical Association, pp. 138 and **Galiano Island Archives website**

[169] **More Tales from the Outer Gulf Islands:** An Anthology of Memories and Anecdotes – British Columbia Historical Association, pp. 273

[170] **More Tales from the Outer Gulf Islands:** An Anthology of Memories and Anecdotes – British Columbia Historical Association, pp. 218 & 273

[171] **Galiano:** Houses And People, Looking back to 1930 – Elizabeth Steward, pp. 27

[172] **More Tales from the Outer Gulf Islands:** An Anthology of Memories and Anecdotes – British Columbia Historical Association, pp. 218 & 273

[173] **Galiano:** Houses And People, Looking back to 1930 – Elizabeth Steward, pp. 27

[174] **Salt Spring Island Archives website:** Details of image 2004026364

[175] **A Gulf Islands Patchwork:** Some Early Events on the Islands of Galiano, Mayne, Saturna, North and South Pender – British Columbia Historical Association, pp. 136 and **Island Heritage Buildings** – Thomas K. Ovanin, Islands Trust, pp. 100

[176] **Homesteads and Snug Harbours:** The Gulf Islands – Peter Murray, pp. 47

[177] **A Gulf Islands Patchwork:** Some Early Events on the Islands of Galiano, Mayne, Saturna, North and South Pender – British Columbia Historical Association, pp. 136

[178] **A Gulf Islands Patchwork:** Some Early Events on the Islands of Galiano, Mayne, Saturna, North and South Pender – British Columbia Historical Association, pp. 136

[179] **A Gulf Islands Patchwork:** Some Early Events on the Islands of Galiano, Mayne, Saturna, North and South Pender – British Columbia Historical Association, pp. 136 & 154

[180] **A Gulf Islands Patchwork:** Some Early Events on the Islands of Galiano, Mayne, Saturna, North and South Pender – British Columbia Historical Association, pp. 136 & 154

Notes

[181] **Homesteads and Snug Harbours:** The Gulf Islands – Peter Murray, pp. 37

[182] **A Gulf Islands Patchwork:** Some Early Events on the Islands of Galiano, Mayne, Saturna, North and South Pender – British Columbia Historical Association, pp. 136 & 154

[183] **Homesteads and Snug Harbours:** The Gulf Islands – Peter Murray, pp. 37

[184] **Island Heritage Buildings** – Thomas K. Ovanin, Islands Trust, pp. 100

[185] **The Gulf Islanders:** Sound Heritage, Volume V, Number 4, pp. 25

[186] **The Historical Pender Islands:** Limited Edition Calendar, 2006 – Pender Islands Museum Society

[187] **The Historical Pender Islands:** Limited Edition Calendar, 2006 – Pender Islands Museum Society

[188] **MayneLiner Magazine:** Volume 13, Number 11, pp. 55

[189] **More Tales from the Outer Gulf Islands:** An Anthology of Memories and Anecdotes – British Columbia Historical Association, pp. 229-231

[190] **More Tales from the Outer Gulf Islands:** An Anthology of Memories and Anecdotes – British Columbia Historical Association, pp. 229-231

[191] **More Tales from the Outer Gulf Islands:** An Anthology of Memories and Anecdotes – British Columbia Historical Association, pp. 229-231

[192] **More Tales from the Outer Gulf Islands:** An Anthology of Memories and Anecdotes – British Columbia Historical Association, pp. 229-231 & 254

[193] **More Tales from the Outer Gulf Islands:** An Anthology of Memories and Anecdotes – British Columbia Historical Association, pp. 229-231

[194] **The Gulf Islanders:** Sound Heritage, Volume V, Number 4, pp. 73

[195] **The Gulf Islanders:** Sound Heritage, Volume V, Number 4, pp. 73

[196] **Southern Gulf Islands**: An Altitude SuperGuide – Spalding, Montgomery and Pitt, pp. 49

[197] **A Gulf Islands Patchwork:** Some Early Events on the Islands of Galiano, Mayne, Saturna, North and South Pender – British Columbia Historical Association, pp. 93

[198] **Homesteads and Snug Harbours:** The Gulf Islands – Peter Murray, pp. 39

[199] **A Gulf Islands Patchwork:** Some Early Events on the Islands of Galiano, Mayne, Saturna, North and South Pender – British Columbia Historical Association, pp. 93

[200] **Homesteads and Snug Harbours:** The Gulf Islands – Peter Murray, pp. 39

[201] **A Gulf Islands Patchwork:** Some Early Events on the Islands of Galiano, Mayne, Saturna, North and South Pender – British Columbia Historical Association, pp. 92

[202] **A Gulf Islands Patchwork:** Some Early Events on the Islands of Galiano, Mayne, Saturna, North and South Pender – British Columbia Historical Association, pp. 93 & 142

[203] **More Tales from the Outer Gulf Islands:** An Anthology of Memories and Anecdotes – British Columbia Historical Association, pp. 147, 192 & 193

Notes

[204] **More Tales from the Outer Gulf Islands:** An Anthology of Memories and Anecdotes – British Columbia Historical Association, pp. 192 & 193

[205] **More Tales from the Outer Gulf Islands:** An Anthology of Memories and Anecdotes – British Columbia Historical Association, pp. 192 & 193

[206] **More Tales from the Outer Gulf Islands:** An Anthology of Memories and Anecdotes – British Columbia Historical Association, pp. 192 & 193

[207] **More Tales from the Outer Gulf Islands:** An Anthology of Memories and Anecdotes – British Columbia Historical Association, pp. 123-129

[208] **More Tales from the Outer Gulf Islands:** An Anthology of Memories and Anecdotes – British Columbia Historical Association, pp. 123-129

[209] **More Tales from the Outer Gulf Islands:** An Anthology of Memories and Anecdotes – British Columbia Historical Association, pp. 123-129

[210] **More Tales from the Outer Gulf Islands:** An Anthology of Memories and Anecdotes – British Columbia Historical Association, pp. 123-129 and **Snapshots of Early Salt Spring and other Favoured Islands:** Mouat's Trading Co. Ltd., pp. 46

[211] **Galiano:** Houses And People, Looking back to 1930 – Elizabeth Steward, pp. 110

[212] **More Tales from the Outer Gulf Islands:** An Anthology of Memories and Anecdotes – British Columbia Historical Association, pp. 123-129 and **Snapshots of Early Salt Spring and other Favoured Islands:** Mouat's Trading Co. Ltd., pp. 46

[213] **More Tales from the Outer Gulf Islands:** An Anthology of Memories and Anecdotes – British Columbia Historical Association, pp. 123-129

[214] **Galiano:** Houses And People, Looking back to 1930 – Elizabeth Steward, pp. 110

[215] **Southern Gulf Islands**: An Altitude SuperGuide – Spalding, Montgomery and Pitt, pp. 21

[216] **Galiano:** Houses And People, Looking back to 1930 – Elizabeth Steward, pp. 115

[217] **Galiano:** Houses And People, Looking back to 1930 – Elizabeth Steward, pp. 115

[218] **The Gulf Islands Explorer:** The Complete Guide – Bruce Obee, pp. 153 & 154

[219] **A Gulf Islands Patchwork:** Some Early Events on the Islands of Galiano, Mayne, Saturna, North and South Pender – British Columbia Historical Association, pp. 9

[220] **Homesteads and Snug Harbours:** The Gulf Islands – Peter Murray, pp. 33

[221] **Homesteads and Snug Harbours:** The Gulf Islands – Peter Murray, pp. 33

[222] **Homesteads and Snug Harbours:** The Gulf Islands – Peter Murray, pp. 17

[223] **A Gulf Islands Patchwork:** Some Early Events on the Islands of Galiano, Mayne, Saturna, North and South Pender – British Columbia Historical Association, pp.139

[224] **A Gulf Islands Patchwork:** Some Early Events on the Islands of Galiano, Mayne, Saturna, North and South Pender – British Columbia Historical Association, pp.139

[225] **Mayne Island Fall Fair:** Centennial Year – Mayne Island Agriculture Society, pp. 21

[226] **Mayne Island Fall Fair:** Centennial Year – Mayne Island Agriculture Society, pp. 21

Notes

[227] **Galiano:** Houses And People, Looking back to 1930 – Elizabeth Steward, pp. 93 and **More Tales from the Outer Gulf Islands:** An Anthology of Memories and Anecdotes – British Columbia Historical Association, pp. 206 & 207

[228] **More Tales from the Outer Gulf Islands:** An Anthology of Memories and Anecdotes – British Columbia Historical Association, pp. 225 & 226

[229] **More Tales from the Outer Gulf Islands:** An Anthology of Memories and Anecdotes – British Columbia Historical Association, pp. 225 & 226

[230] **More Tales from the Outer Gulf Islands:** An Anthology of Memories and Anecdotes – British Columbia Historical Association, pp. 225 & 226

[231] **More Tales from the Outer Gulf Islands:** An Anthology of Memories and Anecdotes – British Columbia Historical Association, pp. 225 & 226

[232] **Snapshots of Early Salt Spring and other Favoured Islands:** Mouat's Trading Co. Ltd., pp. 74 and **More Tales from the Outer Gulf Islands:** An Anthology of Memories and Anecdotes – British Columbia Historical Association, pp. 232

[233] **Snapshots of Early Salt Spring and other Favoured Islands:** Mouat's Trading Co. Ltd., pp. 74 and **More Tales from the Outer Gulf Islands:** An Anthology of Memories and Anecdotes – British Columbia Historical Association, pp. 232

[234] **More Tales from the Outer Gulf Islands:** An Anthology of Memories and Anecdotes – British Columbia Historical Association, pp. 232

[235] **More Tales from the Outer Gulf Islands:** An Anthology of Memories and Anecdotes – British Columbia Historical Association, pp. 232

[236] **Southern Gulf Islands**: An Altitude SuperGuide – Spalding, Montgomery and Pitt, pp. 55

[237] **Galiano:** Houses And People, Looking back to 1930 – Elizabeth Steward, pp. 141

[238] **Galiano:** Houses And People, Looking back to 1930 – Elizabeth Steward, pp. 141

[239] **Galiano:** Houses And People, Looking back to 1930 – Elizabeth Steward, pp. 133

[240] **Homesteads and Snug Harbours:** The Gulf Islands – Peter Murray, pp. 34

[241] **Homesteads and Snug Harbours:** The Gulf Islands – Peter Murray, pp. 34 and **Galiano:** Houses And People, Looking back to 1930 – Elizabeth Steward, pp. 30 & 133

[242] **Homesteads and Snug Harbours:** The Gulf Islands – Peter Murray, pp. 34 and **Galiano:** Houses And People, Looking back to 1930 – Elizabeth Steward, pp. 30 & 133

[243] **Homesteads and Snug Harbours:** The Gulf Islands – Peter Murray, pp. 34 and **Galiano:** Houses And People, Looking back to 1930 – Elizabeth Steward, pp. 133

[244] **Homesteads and Snug Harbours:** The Gulf Islands – Peter Murray, pp. 34

[245] **Homesteads and Snug Harbours:** The Gulf Islands – Peter Murray, pp.41

[246] **Southern Gulf Islands**: An Altitude SuperGuide – Spalding, Montgomery and Pitt, pp. 53

[247] **A Gulf Islands Patchwork:** Some Early Events on the Islands of Galiano, Mayne, Saturna, North and South Pender – British Columbia Historical Association, pp. 144

Notes

[248] **The Terror Of The Coast**: Land Alienation And Colonial War On Vancouver Island And The Gulf Islands – Chris Arnett, pp. 247

[249] **Mayne Island & The Outer Gulf Islands:** A History – Marie Elliott, pp. 89

[250] **Snapshots of Early Salt Spring and other Favoured Islands:** Mouat's Trading Co. Ltd., pp. 66 & 76 and **More Tales from the Outer Gulf Islands:** An Anthology of Memories and Anecdotes – British Columbia Historical Association, pp. 265

[251] **Galiano:** Houses And People, Looking back to 1930 – Elizabeth Steward, pp. 73, 145 & 146

[252] **Galiano:** Houses And People, Looking back to 1930 – Elizabeth Steward, pp. 73, 145 & 146

[253] **Galiano:** Houses And People, Looking back to 1930 – Elizabeth Steward, pp. 73, 145 & 146

[254] **Galiano:** Houses And People, Looking back to 1930 – Elizabeth Steward, pp. 145 & 146

[255] **Homesteads and Snug Harbours:** The Gulf Islands – Peter Murray, pp. 34

[256] **Homesteads and Snug Harbours:** The Gulf Islands – Peter Murray, pp. 34

[257] **Southern Gulf Islands**: An Altitude SuperGuide – Spalding, Montgomery and Pitt, pp. 57

[258] **A Gulf Islands Patchwork:** Some Early Events on the Islands of Galiano, Mayne, Saturna, North and South Pender – British Columbia Historical Association, pp. 17 & 18

[259] **A Gulf Islands Patchwork:** Some Early Events on the Islands of Galiano, Mayne, Saturna, North and South Pender – British Columbia Historical Association, pp. 17 & 18

[260] **A Gulf Islands Patchwork:** Some Early Events on the Islands of Galiano, Mayne, Saturna, North and South Pender – British Columbia Historical Association, pp. 17 & 18

[261] **A Gulf Islands Patchwork:** Some Early Events on the Islands of Galiano, Mayne, Saturna, North and South Pender – British Columbia Historical Association, pp. 17 & 18

[262] **A Gulf Islands Patchwork:** Some Early Events on the Islands of Galiano, Mayne, Saturna, North and South Pender – British Columbia Historical Association, pp. 17 & 18

[263] **A Gulf Islands Patchwork:** Some Early Events on the Islands of Galiano, Mayne, Saturna, North and South Pender – British Columbia Historical Association, pp. 17 & 18

[264] **A Gulf Islands Patchwork:** Some Early Events on the Islands of Galiano, Mayne, Saturna, North and South Pender – British Columbia Historical Association, pp. 17 & 18

[265] **Southern Gulf Islands**: An Altitude SuperGuide – Spalding, Montgomery and Pitt, pp. 51

[266] **Southern Gulf Islands**: An Altitude SuperGuide – Spalding, Montgomery and Pitt, pp. 96

[267] **MayneLiner Magazine:** Volume 15, Number 8, pp. 20

[268] **City of Placerville, California website**

[269] **Salt Spring:** The Story of an Island – Charles Kahn, pp. 201

[270] **Salt Spring:** The Story of an Island – Charles Kahn, pp. 201

Notes

[271] **Salt Spring:** The Story of an Island – Charles Kahn, pp. 201
[272] **Plants of the Pacific Northwest Coast:** Washington, Oregon, British Columbia and Alaska
[273] **Plants of the Pacific Northwest Coast:** Washington, Oregon, British Columbia and Alaska

Index

Index

INdeX

Index

INdeX

INdeX

INdeX